Into the Heart of God

Dear Dyleoo......

You are a gifted young man!
Always put Jesus first & He'll guide
and direct your future. Here's the
secret to become prosperous and
successful... —> "Keep this Book
of the law always on your lips;
meditate on it day & night, so that
you may be careful to do everything
written in it. Then you will be
prosperous & successful." Joshua 1:8

Love you so much!!
aunty Beena
4·1·18

INTO THE HEART OF GOD

Finding Your Destiny in His Presence

A Ninety-Day Journey

DAN CARROLL

Water of Life
community church

Published by Water of Life Community Church
Fontana, California, U.S.A.
www.wateroflifecc.org
Printed in the U.S.A.

Rights for publishing this book outside the U.S.A. or in non-English languages
are administered by Water of Life Community Church. For additional information
please visit www.wateroflifecc.org, e-mail info@wateroflifecc.org, or write to
Water of Life Community Church, 7625 East Avenue, Fontana, CA 92336, U.S.A.

Cover design by Danny Blanton
Interior design by InsideOut CreativeArts

Contents

Preface

Any time we take a journey, we need a guide. You hold in your hand a guide that will help you on your journey of faith. Jesus knew that His disciples would wonder what to do after He left them. That's why He told them a Helper would come. The Holy Spirit will be our guide as we seek to move deeper into the heart of God and let Him change us.

This book is an invitation for you to take a few minutes at the beginning of each day to read and reflect upon a passage of Scripture and what that passage means for you. As you read, please ask God the question, "What do You want to do through my life to extend Your reach into nations and neighborhoods?" If we are to become the people God hungers to make us—people who know God, surrender fully to Him, care for others, and invest in God's kingdom—then meeting with God is crucial for each one of us.

One of the ways I have learned to worship God I wrote about in day 26 of this book:

> Many years ago David's method of worshiping the Lord alone in creation intrigued me so much that I began to spend my mornings on the hillside at the top of Haven Avenue before driving to Pomona to teach school each day. I had no idea that these mornings would shape my destiny. But like David, I found a deep friendship with Jesus when I was outside alone worshiping.

Later I bought a house at the base of the foothills, and to this day I spend most mornings and evenings up the hill communing with God. My favorite hobby is hiking, and I have been blessed to spend a lot of time in the Sierras each summer hiking and praying. It was during one of these times out in creation praying and worshiping that I took the picture on the front cover. You and I both need times of peaceful quiet with the Lord if we are going to go deep into our Father's heart.

The first thirty days of this journey will be devoted to heart preparation. They will be spent around positioning us before God's throne in prayer—honoring God, waiting on Him, and worshiping Him. Take the time to hear what the Spirit of God is saying to you in prayer and in His Word. The second thirty days focus on surrender, courage, faith, risk, obedience. They discuss the obstacles and battles we will encounter as we step out in faith and the tools God has given us to grow in maturity and victory. The last thirty days talk about principles and practices for finding our destiny as we give our lives to God and invest in the work of His kingdom.

When we decide to follow Jesus, we may not know it, but we are deciding several things that will impact our whole lives: we are deciding to walk with Him and not the world; we are deciding to take the time necessary to cultivate a life-giving relationship with Him; we are deciding to let Him teach us His way, which is far different from our ways; and we are deciding to give up our own lives for the furthering of His kingdom. When we sit down with a devotional book like this one, we are entering into a time of impartation, a time when God can speak life into us. Before you begin each day, ask the Holy Spirit to walk with you and build His destiny into your heart. Please take time to be still, to listen to what He has to say to you. This is the only way we can grow in intimacy with Jesus.

God hungers to satisfy our deepest longings and needs—and the only way that can happen is when we grow deep into His heart. He alone has what each of us needs. Many people whose stories we find in the pages of the Bible figured this out and lived close to God's heart. None of them were perfect—which ought to encourage us, because none of us are—but they hungered after their Father's heart in a fashion we all ought to long for. I hope you enjoy the journey into your Father's heart.

Positioning Yourself Before God's Throne

Patient waiting on God is not only beneficial,
but it is often the only way the Lord can work.
If we pick the fruit before it is ripe,
it can completely sidetrack our destiny
in the spiritual realm.

DAY 1

No Relationship Without Time Together

*When you pray, don't be like the hypocrites who love to pray
publicly on street corners and in the synagogues where
everyone can see them. I tell you the truth, that is all the reward
they will ever get. But when you pray, go away by yourself,
shut the door behind you, and pray to your Father in private.
Then your Father, who sees everything, will reward you.*

MATTHEW 6:5-6, NLT

We often think that our relationships will be just fine whether we spend time investing in them or not. But it doesn't take long to figure out that when we neglect relationships, they suffer. It is no different with Jesus. When we invest in relationship with Him, we get life and blessing. When we don't, we suffer. There can be no relationship without conversation and interaction. This is what we call prayer.

Prayer is a lifeline to God. Without prayer there is no relationship. Water of Life has a prayer tower in our worship center with a room at the top overlooking our valley. This room is a key component to all we do to touch others' lives. We have teams of people who pray over all our weekend services and for each of our pastors. Without prayer we will have no breakthrough in our lives and circumstances.

John Wesley, the founder of the Methodist church, once said, "God does nothing on the earth save in answer to believing prayer." Breakthroughs in our lives, whether they are financial, physical, marital, emotional, or spiritual, come through prayer. Communion and intimacy with God come through prayer and conversation with God. In Christ's last days on this earth, during His most trying moments, He used prayer with the Father to calm His Spirit and understand more fully His Father's will. We would all be wise to follow His example.

Instead of running to friends and coworkers for counsel in trying times, why not run to God, bow before Him, and open up to Him? He is there listening to all your needs, and He alone sees everything. Jesus said as much in His teaching on prayer: "When you pray, go away by yourself, shut the door behind you, and pray to your Father in private. Then your Father, who sees everything, will reward you."

‐‐‐‐‐‐‐ PRAYER ‐‐‐‐‐‐‐

Father, teach me to run to You, to pour out my heart to You. So many things crowd my day, and often I am not prayerful. I want to learn the lessons You taught on learning to lean into You first. Holy Spirit, draw me into prayer, praise, and adoration of my Father. Amen.

DAY 2

....

Be Real with God

When you are praying, do not use meaningless repetition as the
Gentiles do, for they suppose that they will be heard for their
many words. So do not be like them; for your Father knows what
you need before you ask Him.

MATTHEW 6:7-8

I am amazed at how many people are afraid to be real with God. This was the key to David's life and love for God. He was real with God. He understood that God knows everything and that even with all that knowledge He is safe to run to, safe to be honest with, safe to share our darkest moments with.

When Jesus taught on prayer, that is exactly what He explained. In Matthew 6:6 He said, "Your Father knows everything." Now "everything" includes everything, doesn't it? All our issues and fears and pain and failures—God knows everything. So why not be real with Him? What do we have to lose? So many of us do exactly what Jesus taught us not do in today's verses. He said, "Do not use meaningless repetition," meaning, "Please forget those rote prayers with no heart that do not reflect reality. I want it real."

But if our Father knows everything, then why talk to Him about it? Relationship. That is why our Father wants us to run to Him and pour out our hearts to Him. He wants relationship with us, real life-giving relationship. Those of us who have children often know what they need long before they tell us, but we want them to grow; we want them to decide to come; we want the relationship that comes from their decision to tell us. Our heavenly Father is just like that.

Do you trust that God is safe? Are you free to be real with Him? He waits for us to come every day and open up our hearts and lives to Him. It is when we do this that we come to know His great love for us. If we don't come to the Father and cast our cares upon Him, the stress of our lives today stacks on top of the stress of yesterday. We don't *have* to pray; we *get* to pray. Personal prayer time every day keeps those blocks of stress from stacking up around us and limiting our vision and hindering our relationship with God.

PRAYER

Jesus, I am sorry that far too much of my time with You isn't intimate and real. Thank You for desiring deep relationship with me. Draw me to Yourself, and teach me to live in Your heart with Your values, not my own. Teach me to come to You daily and set my heart before You, trusting that You are safe and loving. Only then can I be certain that I will fulfill all You have for me. Amen.

DAY 3

....

How Do You Start Your Day?

*In the morning, O LORD, You will hear my voice; in the morning
I will order my prayer to You and eagerly watch.*

PSALM 5:3

I talk to so many people these days who cannot order their private worlds. Their lives consist of internal chaos and external deception. It is hard for us to be real when we aren't honest with ourselves. Internal chaos is like a constant noise that robs us from hearing anything life giving and good. It is loud and hard.

The only way a Christian can survive and flourish is to learn to order his or her private world. By that I mean take the time to let Jesus sort out the noise inside us and around us. We do this by starting our days with prayer and time alone with the Father. I can imagine what many of you are saying: "That would be great, but it is totally unrealistic." Yet many of you will come home and turn on the TV for hours, thinking it will help you unwind. Television does not quiet the chaos inside. Jesus does. Why not try beginning your day by being still for a few minutes? Take the time to do as David said in Psalm 5:3: "In the morning, O LORD, You will hear my voice; in the morning I will order my prayer to You. "

Start your day with the Lord, and order your prayer to Him. If you come to Him in the morning, you can live the rest of the day with a peace that He is in it all. The Hebrew word for "order" means to lay out, to set into rows or set in order. If we are taking the time each morning to "lay out" our days before the Lord, we can then move into our days with confidence that He is in them. This will save us an enormous amount of time and energy fixing all the situations we would have broken if we hadn't spent time with Jesus. When we lay out our lives before Him, we can live each day with an eager anticipation that He will move in us with power and hope, healing and possibility that we could never muster on our own.

Try coming to Him in the morning each day, and see if He doesn't put into you the same heart He gave to David, a heart that will "eagerly watch" for His hand throughout the day.

⟶ PRAYER ⟵

Jesus, there is so much noise in my life today. Will You please quiet my spirit? Holy Spirit, remind me that the time I take to pray in the morning isn't a waste of time but a huge investment in my day. Teach me, Father, to come to You and allow You to touch me with Your peace that will quiet my chaos and the noise that bothers me so much of my day. I hope in You, Father. There is no one like You, Lord. Please move in me with power today. Amen.

....

Your Life Is a Blessing to Your Father

Jesus spoke these things; and lifting up His eyes to heaven,
He said, "Father, the hour has come; glorify Your Son,
that the Son may glorify You."

JOHN 17:1

Some of you don't feel like your life is a blessing to anyone. You may feel lonely, marginalized, and forgotten, but your Father never misses you. Jesus prayed this great prayer in John 17 the last night He would be alive, the day before He would be crucified: "Glorify Your Son, that the Son may glorify You." Could you ever pray a prayer like that? "God, touch me so that I can touch others for You. Touch me so that I can draw near to You and make Your heart smile."

Most of us would be ashamed to pray like this, but Jesus did, and we are supposed to be Christlike. Look how Jesus prayed here. It doesn't say He bowed down or fell on His face, only that He lifted His eyes toward heaven. That is not to say that posture doesn't ever matter, but what it does say is that what is inside, our spiritual hearts, should come out. It is about the heart. Jesus lifted His eyes to where His heart was: heaven.

Now let's be honest. Most of the time when we get up and begin to pray, our hearts aren't set on heavenly things. We must lift our eyes and sometimes our hands and ask God to touch us and awaken His heart in ours. Then we come into the Father's presence as His sons and daughters. Six times in this prayer Jesus called to His Father, because He knew that He was a son, *the* Son. But you and I need the same confidence each day when we come to Him. We come as a son or a daughter loved by our Father, knowing that when we pray and cry out to our Father, He hears us and will meet us.

Psalm 37:4 tells us, "Delight yourself in the LORD; and He will give you the desires of your heart." Find joy in Him today, come to Him today, surrender yourself to Him, and He will meet you at the deepest level. Jesus' desire in His prayer was to glorify the Father. We should want that to be our desire as well, but that will never happen unless we draw near to Him and let Him draw near to us. God is crazy about us and about having relationship with us throughout our days, so dive into Him, and enjoy His life and blessing today!

PRAYER

Father, glorify Yourself in me. Holy Spirit, fill my heart with a deep love for my Father. Teach me to lay down my life for You today, and then please allow me to experience the joy of Your salvation! I want You to have Your way in me today, so I come to You with a great gladness and joy, expecting You to move in me with power today. Thank You, Father! Amen.

DAY 5

....

Ask God to Make You a Giver

You have given him [Jesus] authority over everyone. He gives eternal life to each one you have given him. And this is the way to have eternal life— to know you, the only true God, and Jesus Christ, the one you sent to earth.

JOHN 17:2-3, NLT

It is so easy to let all of life center on us, isn't it? When we do that, we lose our way. Jesus was about ready to die, and yet as He prayed, He prayed for others. That is amazing. God is a giver first and foremost.

Listen to how Jesus prayed. First He said to His Father, "You have given Him authority." God gave Jesus power to touch and heal, redeem and restore, and Jesus wanted to use that authority to touch you and me each day.

Then Jesus prayed about people, saying that the Son "gives eternal life to each one You have given Him." Please notice all the giving going on here. If you know Jesus, you are one of the ones the Father gave to Him, so to you He gives life. Jesus goes on in John 17 naming all the things He gives to the people who know Him: eternal life (17:2), knowledge of the Father (17:6-7), intercession for us (17:9, 20), protection from this world (17:11-12).

God is a giver, and He moves on us to make us givers as well. When we come to the Father in prayer, we often know that we are called to point people to Jesus and not to ourselves or some formula or trick idea, but we need His help in this. It doesn't come naturally. We are sometimes awkward and full of fear in our efforts to share Christ with others. But when we come to pray and are open to God and His ways, He deeply convinces us that there is no other answer to life's questions than Jesus. He actually said that in this prayer when He prayed, "This is the way to have eternal life—to know you, the only true God, and Jesus Christ, the one you sent to earth." If we are to be givers, the single most important thing we can give away each day isn't counsel or money or direction—it is Jesus. Pointing people to Him is the greatest gift we can give.

Make your day a life-giving one. Start by being real with God about your heart and your needs, but don't stop there. Move on and ask Him to give you gifts today, gifts of life and supernatural insight and discernment into people and circumstances. Then when you head out to work or school or shopping, go with Him. Go with confidence that you are His son or daughter and that He alone is the giver of all good gifts (see James 1:17) and that today He wants you to give life to others.

—– P R A Y E R –—

Father, today make me a giver, but only after I have been a receiver. Let me open to You and Your life and power today and receive all that You have for me. Convince me again, Lord, that there is no greater gift I can give people than Jesus. Please impart to me wisdom and insight so that I will know how to touch people with Your heart today. Amen.

DAY 6

Asking Is the Key to the Kingdom

Ask, and it will be given to you.

LUKE 11:9

Nothing great will be accomplished in the kingdom of God unless people who love God stretch out and believe for more. That includes asking God to do more than He may ever have done for us in the past. Jesus' words here are clear: we are to ask of Him. He's telling us to come to the Father, to pursue Him and His will for us. We must ask Him to impart life and insight to us.

We need to decide that we are not going to settle for mediocrity in our Christian lives. God wants us to have more, but we have to ask for it. Asking of God is one condition God puts on advancing His kingdom. He asks people to pray, to believe Him and ask Him to move.

Prayer unlocks unbelievable possibility with God. Psalm 2:8 defines this principle: "Ask of Me, and I will surely give the nations as Your inheritance, and the very ends of the earth as Your possession." In spite of this promise, I think it would be a safe guess that most of us have never claimed a nation for God, never labored over a country believing that He hears the cry of His people and moves with power when we ask.

Today ask the Holy Spirit what nation you should begin to intercede for. Pastor Friday, Water of Life's good friend from Nigeria, e-mails me often asking for prayer for his land that is torn by Islamic terrorists killing Christians. Kenya is another country in need of prayer. Then there are all the other nations Water of Life visits: Cambodia, Thailand, Haiti, Mexico. The list goes on and on.

Adoniram Judson, who impacted much of Burma, said this about prayer for nations: "I never prayed sincerely and earnestly for anything but it came at some time—no matter at how distant a day, somehow, in some shape, probably the last I would have devised, it came." Asking is about pressing into prayer. It is about going after God with our whole hearts, not with vain repetitions, but with a sincere cry of heart. Ask God to give you a deep love for others, and then let that love drive you in prayer for them.

─◌ PRAYER ◌─

Father, give me a deep love for others, a passionate love for those who are lost and hurting, a love like You have for me. Teach me, Holy Spirit, to yield to Your heart and desire for my life. Teach me that my highest calling is to others, not to myself. Thank You for loving me as You do. Your grace and forgiveness toward me are so huge. Amen.

DAY 7

Ask, Seek, and Knock

I say to you, ask, and it will be given to you; seek, and you will find;
knock, and it will be opened to you.

LUKE 11:9

Most of us are good at the first baby step of prayer. It is easy to ask God to do something! Unfortunately, after the asking, we think we are finished; we think that since we have already asked, God does not expect us to do anything more. The first step in any journey is critical; we do need to ask in order to receive. But asking is just the first step. It takes many more steps to continue a real journey of prayer.

Jesus offers His disciples a model for such a prayer journey. Ask, yes, of course! But then we are to seek. And finally, we are to knock on the doors that we come across.

Seeking God's will is much more work than simply asking; seeking takes time, attention, listening, looking, and searching. That journey of prayer will lead us far past asking, deep into new paths of seeking God's way for our lives. Along those paths we will discover doorways—places where choices and decisions must be made. Do we have the courage and commitment to knock on those doors? And when those new doors are opened, will we step into a new way of life?

Simply asking demands little of us. Seeking means searching out God's will for our lives, which will undoubtedly change us and redirect us in God's way. Then knocking on the doors God will open to us may well lead us down paths we never would have imagined!

We do not know what God has in store for us when we begin such a journey, but one thing is certain: such a journey of prayer will change our lives. After all, changing us has always been the real intent of prayer and the heart of God!

One way a person can capture the journey of prayer is by journaling the adventure. During your prayer time, write down what you are asking God for and what He gives you, what you are seeking and what you find, and which doors you knock on and the ones that open to you. This is a great way to build faith. Ask and believe, and see what answers you get as you walk with God in prayer.

—◌ PRAYER ◌—

Lord, I seek Your will and way in my life. Lead me down Your paths for Your name's sake. Open new doors that I might find a new way of life! Give me the courage to allow You to do all You want to do in and through me. Thank You, Jesus. Amen.

DAY 8

....

When You Pray, Don't Give Up!

He was telling them a parable to show that at all times
they ought to pray and not to lose heart. . . . "Will not God bring
about justice for His elect who cry to Him day and night,
and will He delay long over them?"

LUKE 18:1-7

One of the most difficult things about prayer is not seeing an answer immediately. When we pray and pray and wait and wait, it is human nature to begin to doubt. Jesus spoke to this over and over in parables and stories, because He knew human nature and wanted us to press in and stay in and believe beyond what we can see.

Remember the story of Daniel? He prayed and waited and prayed and waited. In Daniel 10 we catch a glimpse of the spiritual realm in Daniel's prayer life when a messenger from heaven spoke to him:

Do not be afraid, Daniel, for from the first day that you set your heart on understanding this and on humbling yourself before your God, your words were heard, and I have come in response to your words. But the prince of the

25

kingdom of Persia was withstanding me for twenty-one days; then behold, Michael, one of the chief princes, came to help me, for I had been left there with the kings of Persia. (Dan. 10:12–14)

Daniel had been praying, seeking, and asking for three weeks, and his prayer had been answered the first day he had asked! The first day! But he hadn't known that, because a battle in the spiritual realm had prevented his answer from becoming reality. How many times have we asked and not seen an answer, so we just gave up? Jesus' parable in Luke 18 is to teach us to stay in, not to give up but to cry out to God, believing that He hears our cry and desires to answer us and *will* answer us.

Prayer is hard. Sometimes what we desire seems impossible. But our prayers make a huge difference in the kingdom of God and in our own lives and destinies. Jesus said in Luke 18:1 that we ought to always pray and not lose heart. So today make a decision that, however difficult you may find prayer, you are going to pray and pray and not lose heart. Ask the Holy Spirit to empower you. He is the Spirit of prayer. He can give you the power to stay in and not lose heart, but you must ask Him.

PRAYER

Father, I want to press into prayer, believing that You will move when I come to You. Teach me the power of prayer. Holy Spirit, fill me with faith and power to stay in and not lose heart when I pray and don't see an answer right away. Thank You, Jesus, that You taught me to pour out my heart to You and that in this I will come to know You more deeply. Amen.

DAY 9

·························

Abide in Jesus for Power in Prayer

If you abide in Me, and My words abide in you,
ask whatever you wish, and it will be done for you.

JOHN 15:7

Jesus made a huge promise in John 15:7: "Ask whatever you wish, and it will be done for you." Wow! If only we knew how to exercise such faith and power, we could change our world, couldn't we? There is no doubt, when we listen to Jesus' words, that the Father has committed Himself to working out all His purposes in us through our prayers. But it is the first part of John 15:7 that leverages the whole promise: *if* we abide in Him and His words abide in us, *then* whatever we ask will be done.

That little word "abide" is *meno* in the original Greek language, and it can be translated into several different English words, including "await," "continue," "dwell," "endures," "lasting," "lives," "remain," "stand," "stay," "tarry," and "wait." All these words have to do with getting in and staying in, pulling close and staying close, abiding in intimacy with Jesus. If we do this and live by His Word, Jesus will birth His heart and will in us. Then when we pray, we will pray the Father's heart for people and situations. When we ask, we will ask with a confidence not born of ourselves but out of God's heart, will, and Word.

Studying the Word and having a handle on God's heart through the Word are crucial for a deep and real prayer life. Many of us pray our emotions—I know I often do, or at least I start there—but it doesn't take long for the Holy Spirit to begin to nudge me into His will, which is most often found in His Word. The Holy Spirit wrote the Bible, so if we want to move deeply in the Spirit, we will have to move deeply in the Word of God. Prayer is essential to a deep life in the believer, and it is attainable when we decide that we would be better served by chasing after God than chasing after the world.

Lay your life down before God, and tell Him that you want to abide with Him and in Him. He will meet you as you seek His face. Stay in. Ask Him to birth consistency in you. He will do it.

—⁀ PRAYER ⁀—

Jesus, teach me what it means to abide in You, to stay close to You, to walk with You. I want more of You—a deeper, life-giving relationship that will empower me to pray. Holy Spirit, You are the great teacher of the Word. I ask You to teach me the Bible. When I read it, speak to my heart. Thank You, Father. Amen.

DAY 10

Effective Prayer

The effective prayer of a righteous man can accomplish much.

JAMES 5:16

James tells us that the effective prayer of a righteous person accomplishes much. When I read that, I kind of sink down inside initially. I think, like you might, "Well, that eliminates me." Words like "righteous" can seem huge and daunting, unattainable and out of reach. But Jesus said in Matthew 6:33 that we are to seek first His kingdom and His righteousness. This principle permeates Scripture. So seeking God's righteousness is important to our prayers.

James certainly saw the significance of Jesus' words when He wrote about prayer. His statement that the effective prayer of a righteous person can accomplish much involves two things we can all embrace.

First, James wrote of prayers that are "effective." Some prayers are effective, and some are not. Prayers or words with no heart mean little to God, but prayers poured out from deep within us are effective. In the next verse, James 5:17, James uses Elijah as an example of a person like us who prayed "earnestly," or literally "prayed with prayer." What? Elijah prayed with prayer. He went for it. He pressed in with all his heart. Elijah's prayer was not an arrow prayer—take aim and shoot and run off to work at the problem on our own. A deep heart conviction drove him.

29

Second, James wrote that these effective prayers are prayed by "a righteous man." What makes a person righteous? When we come to Jesus, we are all made right, or righteous, in Him, but that is not what James is referring to. He is referring to the essence or heart of biblical righteousness, as *The New American Commentary* on James states: "The essence of biblical righteousness is dependence upon God in all one's dealings. To be righteous is to live a life centered upon the word of God; not sinlessness but mercy typifies this life. Indeed, since it is the prayer for others that is being discussed, the righteous are the ones who intercede not so much on behalf of themselves but in obedience to God and for others."[1]

The righteousness James is referring to is a heart after God, one that leans hard into Him and depends on Him, one that seeks Him first, as Jesus said. He's not speaking of a sinless person but one full of mercy and grace who runs to God when he or she falls. Run to God, and be the righteous person only He can shape you into. Then when He calls you to pray for a neighbor or a friend or even a nation, you will be able to pray effectively, with passion.

——◌ PRAYER ◌——

Father, make me an effective prayer warrior, one who loves You and loves others like You do. Put Your heart in me, and fill me, Holy Spirit, with passion when I pray. Teach me what it means to pour out my heart for others so that You can move on them with power. Thank You, Father. Amen.

DAY 11

....

Persistence Pays Off

I tell you, even though he will not get up and give him
anything because he is his friend, yet because of his persistence
he will get up and give him as much as he needs.

LUKE 11:8

When Jesus' disciples asked Him to teach them to pray, He launched into what we call the Lord's Prayer, which is certainly full of prayerful instruction. But then Jesus told a parable, a story, about a man who needed help in the middle of the night. This man had a surprise visitor and had no food to give him. So he went to his neighbor and knocked on his door at midnight. Now you may be a night owl, but this neighbor wasn't. He was asleep along with his family, and he told the guy to beat it, get lost, come back in the morning.

But the man wouldn't take no for an answer. That's the clincher: he kept on asking. He was persistent—the old-school word for this is "importunity." And because of it, finally the neighbor got up and gave the man all he needed. Not because he was his friend, Jesus said, but because of the man's persistence. Jesus then went on to make His great statement about asking, seeking, and knocking in Luke 11:9–10: "So I say to you, ask, and it will be given to you; seek, and you will find; knock, and it will be opened to you. For everyone who asks, receives; and he who seeks, finds; and to him who knocks, it will be opened."

The message is pretty clear: persistence matters. Why? Well, persistence makes a lot of statements, such as "God will meet me" and "Spiritual warfare may slow down my prayers, but it won't defeat them" and "I have nowhere else to go to get what I need, so I will keep coming to my Father."

One of the biggest things persistence declares is that we believe in a spiritual realm, so we press into it even though we can't see what is taking place there. This is where Elijah was in 1 Kings 18. Following a great drought in the land, Elijah prayed for rain, but nothing happened. Seven times he sent his servant to look at the sky while he prayed, and six times the servant came back and told him, "There is nothing." Elijah told him to check again, and finally, the seventh time, the servant told him, "Behold, a cloud as small as a man's hand is coming up from the sea" (1 Kings 18:44). After six times of failure, the seventh time there came a huge rain.

We have to press into God and believe that He will come. Don't give up. Don't grow discouraged. Ask the Lord to refine your prayer into His prayer, but don't give up. Let Him reprove you and shape you and mold your prayer life. Stay in with Him, and He will move mountains through you.

PRAYER

Father, teach me that persistence matters. In our day and age, only expedience matters, but I am learning that in spiritual matters I must allow You, Holy Spirit, to teach me. Your ways are not my ways; they are higher and better than mine. Thank You for loving me, Father. Amen.

DAY 12

....

Waiting Is Hard

I wait quietly before God, for my victory comes from him.
He alone is my rock and my salvation,
my fortress where I will never be shaken.

PSALM 62:1-2, NLT

Don't you hate waiting? Whether it's in line at the grocery store, looking for a parking spot, or sitting on the freeway, waiting is the worst! One summer I drove through the Cajon Pass one afternoon, and little did I know that there was a fire up the road in the median between the northbound and southbound lanes. That twelve-mile trip took me one and a half hours! Anyone who has lived in Los Angeles for any length of time knows what I am talking about.

Why is it that the Bible talks over and over about waiting on God? What could God do for a person who spent his or her life waiting on Him? I think that person would probably change the world. Waiting is investing time, not wasting it. When we invest wisely, we always get a good return. Psalm 62 tells us that the person who is waiting is believing for victory in life. Who doesn't want victory? But which of us is willing to go to God and set our case before Him and then wait?

Waiting says something very important to God: "There is nowhere else to go but to You, my Father." Not waiting also says something. It says, "I don't believe that God will do it." Psalm 62:2 makes it really clear that there is nowhere to go for our answers but to God: "He alone is my rock and my salvation." God alone can save us. We don't figure this out overnight. We only get it if we keep coming to God and believing Him to move in our circumstances. It is when we wait that we receive, not when we run off to do something that keeps us busy.

This is a huge fundamental principle. We are needy—we need hope; we need life; we need direction and healing. These are needs only Jesus can fill, but He only fills them when we wait on Him, when we sit still with Him and let Him speak to us. This is basic living in Jesus. Learn to take time to receive from Him the victory you need.

—◌ PRAYER ◌—

Father, everything about waiting is hard. It is hard to stop, hard to stay still. The world travels fast today, and waiting is just so difficult. And if I don't look to You in my waiting, being patient is impossible. Please meet me as I wait for You. Please show up and touch me with Your heart. Thank You for teaching me that waiting can be life giving and healing, Lord. Amen.

DAY 13

....

God Keeps His Word

The LORD took note of Sarah as He had said, and the LORD did for Sarah as He had promised. So Sarah conceived and bore a son to Abraham in his old age, at the appointed time of which God had spoken to him. Abraham called the name of his son who was born to him, whom Sarah bore to him, Isaac.

GENESIS 21:1-3

Abraham and Sarah waited thirty years! That seems totally unreasonable, doesn't it? God, why thirty years? But Jesus is never wrong, and the Scriptures tell us it was the appointed time—not too soon and not too late. Notice how the emphasis in these verses tells us that the Lord did as He had promised. This is so important for us to grasp. Jesus keeps His word.

We often think waiting is wasted time—far from it. It is time invested into eternity. Jesus told His followers in Acts 1:4, "Wait for the gift my Father promised" (NIV). Their waiting allowed the Holy Spirit to touch them; our waiting does the same.

Waiting on God is so difficult, but almost every story in the Word has an issue of timing. Timing is crucial to God and to us. The key is not to give up our faith; we need to wait and keep waiting. We must stay before God, in His presence daily. Romans 4:18–22 tells us how important this is:

In hope against hope he [Abraham] believed, so that he might become a father of many nations according to that which had been spoken, "So shall your descendants be." Without becoming weak in faith he contemplated his own body, now as good as dead since he was about a hundred years old, and the deadness of Sarah's womb; yet, with respect to the promise of God, he did not waver in unbelief but grew strong in faith, giving glory to God, and being fully assured that what God had promised, He was able also to perform. Therefore it was also credited to him as righteousness.

When God has you waiting, wait in faith. How do you know if you're waiting in faith? Look at Abraham—he waited in faith, not wavering in unbelief but growing strong in faith and giving glory to God. Can you give glory to God while you are waiting?

Believe this: God is after you, and waiting on Him allows you to be positioned to be touched deeply by Him. No wasted time there! Don't rush in; God hasn't forgotten you. He knows your address, and He is on the way. He appoints the time, and His time is right: "For the vision is yet for the appointed time; it hastens toward the goal and it will not fail. Though it tarries, wait for it; for it will certainly come, it will not delay" (Hab. 2:3).

PRAYER

Jesus, I am so impatient sometimes. Please forgive me. Teach me to wait on You and not just to wait but to wait in faith, giving glory to You. Holy Spirit, I need You to work this out in me. It often seems impossible, and on my own I know it is. But You can do it. Thank You! Amen.

DAY 14

....

Trust God's Timing

It happened at the end of two full years that Pharaoh had a dream.

GENESIS 41:1

Joseph spent at least ten years waiting for God to rescue him. He must have been wounded at times by the long delays. He once asked a man to help him (see Gen. 40), but the man forgot Joseph and left him in prison for two more years. It seems there was no justice here. But God was in it all.

Waiting is hard, but the pain of waiting is usually part of our growing process. It is always meant for good. Could Pharaoh have had his dream two years earlier? Yes, but God set Himself to work in Joseph at deep levels so that Joseph would be a man He could use greatly. A. W. Tozer said, "It is doubtful whether God can bless a man greatly until he has hurt him deeply." We can never know what God is up to inside us, healing, restoring, and redeeming our lives and destinies. Remain still, and keep believing that He will show up. He hasn't forgotten you or your need.

So much of life in Christ is spent waiting, allowing Him to refine us. It often feels as if we have been forgotten, but as Job reminds us, God never forgets us: "He knows the way I take; when He has tried me, I shall come forth as gold. My foot has held fast to His path; I have kept His way and not turned aside. I have not departed from the command of His lips; I have treasured the words of His mouth more than my necessary food" (Job 23:10–12).

Joseph endured so much. Any time I think of Joseph, I think of the tenderness of brokenness, how God allows us to end up with "a broken spirit; a broken and a contrite heart" (Ps. 51:17). But when we are in the fire, God is watching over us. He watched Joseph, and He watches us, longing to restore and mend and touch us. And yes, He uses pain and brokenness to do that. Our brokenness is not weakness—never think that. It is possibility for destiny. It provides God a great opportunity to work in us.

We can never know the day or the hour when the Holy Spirit might move to rescue us. When Joseph came before Pharaoh, he was a different man than he had been two years before that. When Pharaoh asked Joseph if he could interpret his dreams as he had been told, Joseph told him the truth: "It is not in me" (Gen. 41:16). Joseph had figured out that it was all about God, not him, and that God's Spirit was at work in him to do great things.

God is at work in you both to will and to do according to the riches of His glory (see Phil. 2:13). Be still and let Him have His way, and He will free you and deliver you at just the right time.

—✑ PRAYER ✑—

Dear Lord, teach me to wait until You are done working. I know that You are at work in me doing a great thing. Thank You for being so faithful to me. I trust You to do all you have promised, in Your time, by Your Holy Spirit. Amen.

DAY 15

....

Waiting for Instructions

Make me know Your ways, O LORD; teach me Your paths.
Lead me in Your truth and teach me, for You are the God of my
salvation; for You I wait all the day.

PSALM 25:4-5

If we realized more often how much pain we could avoid by waiting for God to instruct us, I bet we would actually begin to enjoy
waiting on Him. It isn't unusual for most of us to hurry into our
days, only to get blown up somewhere along the way. A cross word,
a jealous attitude, an angry reply can set us off when we are not
prepared inside for the battle each day brings.

The only way we can learn to live without losing our way is to
wait for God to instruct us each day. "Make me know Your ways, O
LORD; teach me Your paths" tells us that there are His ways and our
ways, His paths and our paths. It is easy for us to follow our own
paths, but that usually doesn't get us where we really want to go.
In fact, when we don't allow the Lord to instruct our way, we often
end up bankrupt inside, hurt, angry, or offended.

In Psalm 25:12-13 David goes on to say that the one who receives instruction from God is the one whose soul will abide in
prosperity. The word "prosperity" in the Hebrew language can
mean "good," "merry," "agreeable," "pleasant" or "beautiful."[2]

That is way better than the results our own bankrupt choices bring about. But the only way we can abide in prosperity is if we wait.

Jesus spoke about the importance of waiting on the Lord in Luke 12:35-38 when He talked about the need to be ready for His return. He said,

> Be dressed for service and keep your lamps burning, as though you were waiting for your master to return from the wedding feast. Then you will be ready to open the door and let him in the moment he arrives and knocks. The servants who are ready and waiting for his return will be rewarded. I tell you the truth, he himself will seat them, put on an apron, and serve them as they sit and eat! He may come in the middle of the night or just before dawn. But whenever he comes, he will reward the servants who are ready. (NLT)

Be ready while you are waiting! Learn to wait with expectation that God will show up, because Jesus says that He will not only show up but will reward those who wait expectantly. This actually makes waiting a blessing. It becomes a bit like Christmas. We hate the wait, but it is worth it on Christmas morning! Waiting on the Lord builds anticipation of a great move of God in and through us. That, my friend, is worth waiting for in prayer today.

—⌾ PRAYER ⌾—

Father, waiting holds the key to so many things. Teach me to enjoy waiting before You. Fill me, Lord, with anticipation that You are building something in me worth waiting for. Thank You, Father, that Your ways work even when I don't always understand them. Amen.

....

Waiting Will Change Your Destiny

Rest in the LORD and wait patiently for Him. . . .
For evildoers will be cut off, but those who wait for the LORD,
they will inherit the land.

PSALM 37:7-9

Anyone who has been around Water of Life Community Church for any length of time knows that several verses in Psalm 37 changed my life and the life of our church. We never know when we will be in a season of instruction from the Lord, but we will have a way better idea of what God is up to if we are still and wait for Him to speak.

In 1997 a lady gave me Psalm 37:7-11 and told me, "The Lord has a word for you." A lot of people give me words that they believe are from God, and I pray over them and wait to see if they are in fact from Him. This particular word struck me deeply and just wouldn't go away. It was truly from the Lord. But who is really happy about a word that tells you to wait? I wasn't. But I did wait and trust, and later we did inherit the land, the land on East Avenue. We made the down payment with the money that a woman named Helen Lovett left to Water of Life in her will—our inheritance from the Lord.

Patient waiting on God is not only beneficial, but it is often the only way the Lord can work. If we pick the fruit before it is ripe, it can completely sidetrack our destiny in the spiritual realm. When God kept allowing Water of Life to run into dead-end roads while looking for a new property, I was able to survive when others began to be critical of our lack of success. God allowed us to run into one cul-de-sac after another, but He was in it all and had a perfect plan for us to build our new sanctuary on East Avenue in 2015.

How do you handle waiting? Do you wait patiently in faith? Or do you lose your heart and your hope? Patient waiting precludes fretting. It means allowing the Holy Spirit to walk us through each day until the time is right for a breakthrough. Water of Life waited seven years to build a new worship center. Was that an accident? Never. There are no accidents in Jesus, only blessings for those who wait. Because of the delay, we sold a piece of land on Sierra Avenue for 21 million dollars that we had bought for only 5 million dollars a couple years earlier.

Are we blessed? Yes, but we waited and waited. Is God good? Yes, but He was good when we had nothing from Him but instructions to wait. Stay in with God, and He will meet you.

─◌ PRAYER ◌─

Father, convince me that waiting can give me life. Help me learn not to fret and get so uptight when I don't see You moving. Teach me to wait patiently and hopefully. Thank You, Father, that You never forget or lose sight of me. Amen.

DAY 17

....

Your Times Have Been Appointed

The vision is yet for the appointed time; it hastens toward
the goal and it will not fail. Though it tarries, wait for it;
for it will certainly come, it will not delay.

HABAKKUK 2:3

Does it ever occur to you that God—yes, God Almighty, the Creator of the heavens and earth—has appointed times and seasons in our lives and destinies? Many of us, if we were honest, would say no, we either don't believe it or we don't trust Him enough to wait for His times. We encourage people to walk with God, but let's be honest—God walks slowly, sometimes really slowly, and it can be tough to keep pace with Him. But waiting for Him is essential to fulfilling our destinies.

God may be slow, but He is always on time. "The vision is yet for the appointed time"—that word "appointed" means a fixed or definite time or season in Hebrew. God has these set times for all of us, times we would rather not wait for and often cannot understand the need to wait for. But appointed times from God are just that—appointed from God! Think about that for a minute. If you knew that God loved you so much that He would watch your life and calendar so He could send you an answer at just the right time, wouldn't that make a difference in your waiting?

What if we believed that God was eager to give us what we need but still takes His time? The Bible teaches that He is eager and willing to meet us yet does not hurry: "The LORD longs to be gracious to you, and therefore He waits on high to have compassion on you. For the LORD is a God of justice; how blessed are all those who long for Him" (Isa. 30:18). Take a minute and let that verse sink in, would you? How can the Lord long for anything and yet wait for it? But that is exactly what Isaiah 30:18 teaches us. God has appointed times for us that He longs to release in our lives, but He waits on high for the right time.

Everything is in Christ's timing. Learn to wait; learn to believe that God will come through. Stay in during the good seasons and the bad, and you will see His hand move and your destiny released.

‚ PRAYER ‚

Lord, I need to know You better and understand Your ways more. Please help me be more patient. Teach me that waiting opens the doors for blessing. Remind me when I am impatient that Your seasons are what I need and Your appointed times are always the right times. Amen.

DAY 18

....

Waiting for Righteousness

*We through the Spirit, by faith, are waiting for
the hope of righteousness.*

GALATIANS 5:5

Most of us who have been Christians for very long know the value of being Spirit led. When we allow the Holy Spirit to lead and guide us, life works, and power flows to touch lives. When we live in our own power, or in the flesh, life gets bumpy in a hurry. Galatians 5:5 tells us that if we live by the Spirit, we will eagerly wait in hope by faith for God's hand to move. The word for "waiting" here in Greek doesn't just mean to wait; it is a combination of two words and means to wait eagerly, hopefully, expectantly for righteousness.

You might be saying, "What does that have to do with my daily life?" Well, Paul is actually contrasting lifestyles here: those who work to please God and operate in the flesh with little faith and those who wait on God and move in the Spirit and live out of faith. Those who live in faith learn to wait rather than work their way to God. They understand that Jesus did all the work on the cross, and in order to be successful in life, they need to lean into Him, not themselves. Our lives are not to be about our work but about the overflow that comes from waiting on God.

"The hope of righteousness" is the hope of the cross, us being made right with God not by our effort but by faith, which often manifests in waiting. When we wait on the Lord, we are telling Him that we believe He has all we need. We come to Him eagerly and expectantly, knowing that He will daily make us right with Him. If we need correction, He will give it; if we need hope, He will impart it; if we need healing, He has it. So we come expectantly and wait. We wait for His timing, His direction, His movement.

When life gets dark and depressing and the sky seems to be falling, come to Him and wait in hope. When your joy is gone and your victory seems lost, tell Him, "I will wait eagerly for You. Give me the strength to be still and to believe that if You are for me, no one can stand against me." Great strength comes to those who wait in hope.

PRAYER

Father, waiting in hope sometimes seems impossible. But I know that in You all things are possible. Holy Spirit, please encourage me as I learn to wait, not in anxiety and despair, not in restlessness and frustration, but in hope. Thank You, Lord. Amen.

DAY 19

Patient Waiting Is Crucial to Growth

I waited patiently for the LORD.

PSALM 40:1

When we study the life of David, it is amazing to see how many times he visited this topic of waiting on the Lord. Wait, wait, wait. David had watched King Saul fail miserably because he never learned to wait on the Lord. It was Saul's weakest point as a leader, and his inability in this area led to his downfall as king. Anyone can charge ahead and take matters into his or her own hands. But waiting for the Lord to move while not being in control, not holding the steering wheel, shipwrecks most of us.

Let's consider the consequences of Saul's not waiting. The story is found in 1 Samuel 13:8–14:

> He waited seven days, according to the appointed time set by Samuel, but Samuel did not come to Gilgal; and the people were scattering from him. So Saul said, "Bring to me the burnt offering and the peace offerings." And he offered the burnt offering. As soon as he finished offering the burnt offering, behold, Samuel came; and Saul went out to meet him and to greet him. But Samuel said, "What have you done?" And Saul said, "Because I saw that the

> people were scattering from me, and that you did not come within the appointed days, and that the Philistines were assembling at Michmash, therefore I said, 'Now the Philistines will come down against me at Gilgal, and I have not asked the favor of the LORD.' So I forced myself and offered the burnt offering." Samuel said to Saul, "You have acted foolishly; you have not kept the commandment of the LORD your God, which He commanded you, for now the LORD would have established your kingdom over Israel forever. But now your kingdom shall not endure. The LORD has sought out for Himself a man after His own heart, and the LORD has appointed him as ruler over His people, because you have not kept what the LORD commanded you."

Now Saul did wait seven days, which is a long time when you have people pressuring you. But he didn't wait until the time was fulfilled, or full. He watched his people, full of fear, scattering, and he did what we have all done: he panicked and, as he said, "forced" himself. But his inability to wait cost him the throne. Interestingly enough, it is here that we first hear the phrase that God will have "a man after His own heart." Note the difference between a person after God's heart and one who is not: he or she is willing to wait.

PRAYER

Lord, I know that wise people learn from others' mistakes. Help me learn from Saul's failure to wait. I want to understand the value that waiting has in the kingdom of God. Show me how vital it is to all You can and will do through me. Father, I bow down today and ask You to teach me to learn the lesson of waiting. Thank You. Amen.

DAY 20

....

God Meets Those Who Wait for Him

How blessed is he who keeps waiting.

DANIEL 12:12

It is hard to connect with God a lot of the time. But those who have learned the value of waiting have figured out that if we wait on Him, He will come. He always does if we are still and expectant. Will it take time? Of course, but it is well worth the wait when God shows up. Daniel was prophesying about the end of time when he wrote, "How blessed is he who keeps waiting." Is there any one of us who doesn't want God to bless him or her? The one who keeps waiting—not the one who starts but the one who keeps it up—will not be disappointed.

To keep waiting we have to settle several issues. First, God is fundamentally good. He is crazy about us; He loves us deeply. He wants to bless us if we will come to Him.

Second, God is not playing games with us but building destiny in us. Cynical hearts have no place in the kingdom. When our hearts begin to grow cynical, we should ask ourselves why. We may be losing faith, we may have been wounded, our expectations may be out of order—any number of things may be wrong. But we must not allow cynicism to grow when God asks us to wait, because it poisons our hearts. God always has a good reason for what He does.

When Jesus heard that Lazarus was sick, He waited two days to start traveling to his home:

The sisters sent word to Him, saying, "Lord, behold, he whom You love is sick." But when Jesus heard this, He said, "This sickness is not to end in death, but for the glory of God, so that the Son of God may be glorified by it." Now Jesus loved Martha and her sister and Lazarus. So when He heard that he was sick, He then stayed two days longer in the place where He was. (John 11:3–6)

We couldn't imagine a more confusing response to this family's pain. They waited in grief, loss, and great sadness, but Jesus let them wait. The seeming message is that He didn't care, which is just what we think when God makes us wait—but that is completely inaccurate. Don't surrender to that mentality. Believe that God will come in His timing, and His timing will be perfect.

Third, to keep waiting we must believe that God is working, even when we cannot see what He is doing. He is arranging things exactly as they are supposed to be. When you don't know what to do, position yourself before the Lord, pour out your heart, and wait. He will bless you! When it seems impossibly long, stay in; don't give up. He will come and save you. Remember, waiting shows that we believe His will is more important than ours. It declares, "Not my will, but Yours be done" (Luke 22:42).

─◌ PRAYER ◌─

Father, I cannot know why You make me wait, especially when it seems so wrong to my circumstances and situations. But thank You that when I do wait, I end up being blessed. Please teach me to wait without growing doubtful or cynical or hard. Help me wait in faith and expectation. Amen.

DAY 21

....

When You Hurt, Wait on God

To You, O Lord, I lift up my soul. O my God, in You I trust,
do not let me be ashamed; do not let my enemies exult over me.
Indeed, none of those who wait for You will be ashamed; those who deal
treacherously without cause will be ashamed. Make me know Your
ways, O Lord; teach me Your paths. Lead me in Your truth and teach me,
for You are the God of my salvation; for You I wait all the day.

PSALM 25:1–5

David wrote many psalms, but none gives us more insight into his heart than Psalm 25. It was written in David's latter years and is full of wisdom and truth. David, like us, often felt pained and battered. His heart was large but also bruised. He learned early in his life to call on the Lord and wait patiently and hopefully for Him to move. This psalm speaks to these things. If you are in need, dive into Psalm 25, for you will find God there. In the twenty-two verses that make up this psalm, three times David talks about those who wait on the Lord and about how those who wait get their needs met (see Ps. 25:3, 5, 21).

Is God good? Even if He makes us wait? David declares that He is: "Do not remember the sins of my youth or my transgressions; according to Your lovingkindness remember me, for Your goodness' sake, O Lord. Good and upright is the Lord. . . . All the paths of the LORD are lovingkindness and truth" (Ps. 25:7–10). Is a hard, cynical heart dangerous? Verse 9 answers that: "He leads the humble in justice, and He teaches the humble His way." Should we trust that His hand is working even if we cannot see it? David indicates so:

> The secret of the LORD is for those who fear Him, and He will make them know His covenant. My eyes are continually toward the LORD, for He will pluck my feet out of the net. Turn to me and be gracious to me, for I am lonely and afflicted. The troubles of my heart are enlarged; bring me out of my distresses. . . . Guard my soul and deliver me; do not let me be ashamed, for I take refuge in You. Let integrity and uprightness preserve me, for I wait for You. (Ps. 25:14–21)

If life is hard and your heart is hurting, lay out your life before God. He is there, and He is listening. Sit before Him and wait. He will move on you with hope and life, power and possibility. He is crazy about you!

—꿈 PRAYER 꿈—

Father, You have made it clear that Your heart is for me. I am sorry that so often I need You to convince me that You love me. Teach me that waiting is good and life giving. It is not an indication of a lack of love but of a deep love. Thank You. Amen.

DAY 22

Faith Develops Through Waiting

My soul, wait in silence for God only, for my hope is from Him.
He only is my rock and my salvation, my stronghold; I shall not be
shaken. On God my salvation and my glory rest; the rock of my
strength, my refuge is in God. Trust in Him at all times, O people;
pour out your heart before Him; God is a refuge for us.

PSALM 62:5-8

David understood more than most of us can imagine that for faith to grow and mature, we must learn to wait. He says, "My soul, wait in silence for God only, for my hope is from Him." This is crucial to our well-being. David says that he waits for a reason: his hope is from God. Most of us would say, as David did, that our hope comes from God, but in truth we hope in so many other things today—stuff, technology, science. All of these offer us life and hope at some level, certainly more than they did in David's day, but they are not our answer.

It is difficult to fix our hope on Jesus in our day. We are so distracted. Most of us don't even realize it. But when things distract us from hoping in God, we get ourselves in huge trouble. Faith waits on God. To wait on Him and in Him is the posture of faith. To wait in silence today is pretty tough for many of us. Quiet actually scares some people in our day because we are so used to dealing with noise inside and out. But the salvation of the Lord comes to those who set Him as their rock, their stronghold.

Jesus is our rock, our salvation. He alone is our refuge in times of need. As David said in verse 8, "Trust in Him at all times, O people; pour out your heart before Him; God is a refuge for us." We must trust in Him at *all* times, not just when it is comfortable or safe; then we will find that He becomes our refuge. We need to pour out our hearts to Him. I encourage people to do this all the time, and I often get pushback like, "I don't think He really wants to hear it all." Oh my, read your Bible. Pour out your heart. God knows all that is in it, but He hungers for relationship with us, so He asks us to come to Him and pour out our hearts. Look around at those who are growing in Jesus and have a deep love for God. These people have figured this out.

Pour out your heart! Tell the Lord everything, every fear and every thrill. Tell Him when you are angry and full of doubt. Tell Him, and watch Him work. Come to Him; wait on Him; pour out your heart to Him. He will not disappoint you.

—◌ PRAYER ◌—

Jesus, teach me how vital it is for me to be totally honest with You—to share with You my ups and my downs, the good and the bad. I want more of You, and I see that for me to grow, You must get more of me. Remind me how important honesty is in my relationship with You. Thank You, Lord. Amen.

DAY 23

....

Honoring the Sabbath

There remains a Sabbath rest for the people of God.
For the one who has entered His rest has himself also rested from
his works, as God did from His. Therefore let us be diligent to
enter that rest, so that no one will fall, through following the
same example of disobedience.

HEBREWS 4:9-11

The chaotic and hectic nature of our lives today demands that we set aside a day each week to come before God with our burdens and lay them at His feet. The Sabbath is a much-needed medicine for our physical, mental, and spiritual health. We must not let life sweep us up and race us right past the very thing we need to sustain and strengthen us.

A few years ago I found myself completely burned out. I was contemplating leaving the ministry and moving on to something else. I couldn't see how the life I was living could be from God. I was tired and grouchy. Fortunately, I called a couple friends of mine who were pastors and shared my story with them. They both gave me the same counsel: "Don't leave the ministry, but do honor God and rest."

Rest sometimes seems like lost time, especially if we are type A people. It can make us feel guilty and like someone who doesn't care about others, but this is all bad thinking born from a culture that prides itself on doing life its own way. God's way isn't like this at all. God's way has rest built in—a Sabbath day, a day to stop and recover. It is found all over the Bible, in the Old Testament and in the New Testament.

God made people, and He knows what we need more than we do. We are prideful, and we tend to discount God's directives, thinking that we are smarter than He is or that His instructions are for weak people. But the truth is, our Father knows best. We need a Sabbath each week. If we go without one, we will begin to slowly pay the price. Jesus was clear about His life in us: it should bear the marks of a Sabbath rest: "Come to Me, all who are weary and heavy laden, and I will give you rest. Take My yoke upon you and learn from Me, for I am gentle and humble in heart, and you will find rest for your souls. For My yoke is easy and My burden is light" (Matt. 11:28–30).

Be wise and stop one day each week, and watch what your heavenly Father will do to renew and refresh you. He will bless you and add back into your week time you never thought you could have.

—◌ PRAYER ◌—

Father, I live in a world that rolls right past the Sabbath day each week. Our culture has made every day a day to make money, and I feel so guilty if I stop to rest. Remind me that You have called me out of the world into Your life and that Your life includes rest. Thank You, Jesus, that You know far better than I do what I really need to be a success in this world. Amen.

DAY 24

....

Waiting Imparts Strength and Possibility

Do you not know? Have you not heard? The Everlasting God, the LORD,
the Creator of the ends of the earth does not become weary or tired.
His understanding is inscrutable. He gives strength to the weary,
and to him who lacks might He increases power. Though youths grow
weary and tired, and vigorous young men stumble badly, yet those
who wait for the LORD will gain new strength; they will mount up with
wings like eagles, they will run and not get tired, they will walk and
not become weary.

ISAIAH 40:28–31

This text in Isaiah 40 certainly ranks as one of the greatest in all of Scripture. It is a picture of contrast: God and man, strength and weakness, the world and the Spirit. Here God stands above all else with Isaiah asking, "Have you not heard? God is God. He is not a man. He is God, and He is all-powerful. He lacks neither strength nor wisdom for those who will come and wait on Him. He understands everything—yes, everything. He is God!"

But there is more here than just the greatness of God. There is His desire to impart His power and possibility to people! Yes, people like you and me who will come to Him and wait on Him. It is God who gives strength to the weary and tired. He will impart possibility that we can get nowhere else.

Why don't we settle the issue of waiting today? When we wait on the Lord, He will do great and mighty things in us and for us and with us. When we wait on the Lord, He will refresh us and renew us. He will impart new strength to us, a strength both inward and outward.

Are you weak spiritually? Wait on Him for new strength. Are you weary physically? Stop, take a day off, a Sabbath day, and wait on the Lord and see if He doesn't honor you by refreshing you. Some of us will argue, "I can't afford to take a day off," when in actuality you can't afford not to. Your insistence to keep going is actually a demonstration of a lack of faith. You believe that you make your life work more than Jesus does. You believe that you sustain yourself more than God does. Hmmm, not very smart. Take a day off and sit before the Lord. Wait on Him to renew your strength, and watch what He can do.

PRAYER

Father, forgive me for being stubborn and foolish sometimes. When I think I can run my life better than You can, I always get into trouble. Teach me, Holy Spirit, to stop and wait. Remind me that waiting isn't lost time but a great investment. Thank You, Lord. Amen.

DAY 25

....

Worship Is Vital to Your Destiny

O God, you are my God; I earnestly search for you.
My soul thirsts for you; my whole body longs for you in this
parched and weary land where there is no water. I have seen you
in your sanctuary and gazed upon your power and glory.
Your unfailing love is better than life itself; how I praise you!
I will praise you as long as I live, lifting up my hands to you in prayer.

PSALM 63:1-4, NLT

Our days are consumed with busyness. We are wired up, our phones are on, and life hits us as soon as we open our eyes. When one thousand people were asked what they would do if they had an extra hour added to their day, the overwhelming majority of them said they would relax or sleep![3] Wow, we must be tired people. It is easy to get caught in the madness, but the results are often devastating for us and those around us.

Jesus had a better way. When He was on the earth, He didn't heal or meet or talk to everybody, yet when He went to the cross, He declared, "It is finished!" (John 19:30). He didn't try to do everything, yet He completed all He had come to do. The same challenge faces you and me every day: will we complete our missions here on Earth or just be extremely busy all our lives?

David realized that worship was the main thing—not an afterthought in a busy life. His greatness was born out of that. We too were made to worship, and if we are to fulfill our highest and best purpose in this life, we need to figure this out. Worship isn't an option; it is a must. Do you ever stop and just speak out to the Lord, "How I praise You! There is no one like You"? If we are going to develop hearts after God, we must learn that worship and praise are vital to our lives.

Jesus was clear about this:

> As soon as He was approaching, near the descent of the Mount of Olives, the whole crowd of the disciples began to praise God joyfully with a loud voice for all the miracles which they had seen, shouting: "Blessed is the King who comes in the name of the Lord; peace in heaven and glory in the highest!" Some of the Pharisees in the crowd said to Him, "Teacher, rebuke Your disciples." But Jesus answered, "I tell you, if these become silent, the stones will cry out!" (Luke 19:37-40)

Start your day with your heart set before God, not with your phone going off. Worship Him, praise Him, and watch how He brings life to your day.

—◌ PRAYER ◌—

Father, teach me to worship You, to speak out my praise for You. So many things crowd my day, and often I am not worshipful. I want to learn the lessons you taught David. I want to be after Your heart, and I know that begins with worship. Holy Spirit, draw me into praise and adoration of my Father. Amen.

DAY 26

....

Becoming a Worshiper

The LORD has sought out for Himself a man after His own heart.

1 SAMUEL 13:14

Walking with God is a daily event, sometimes thrilling and sometimes not. When we awake each morning, we have no idea what the day will hold, but, as we often say, we know who holds the day.

The first time David was mentioned in the Bible, it says that God was seeking a man who was seeking after Him. It describes David as a man after God's own heart. At that time David was a young man, likely in his early teens, yet he had already established a pattern of worship—a pattern that marks all seventy-three of the psalms he wrote.

David built his lifestyle of worship alone on the hillsides of Bethlehem, during the years he was tending the sheep for his father. Many years ago David's method of worshiping the Lord alone in creation intrigued me so much that I began to spend my mornings on the hillside at the top of Haven Avenue before driving to Pomona to teach school each day. I had no idea that these mornings would shape my destiny. But like David, I found a deep friendship with Jesus when I was outside alone worshiping.

When my wife and I were looking to purchase a home, I prayed and asked the Lord for a place where I could walk with Him outside each day. I knew I couldn't afford to live at the top of Haven, but I also knew that Jesus could make a way where there was no way. A short time after this, a friend told me of a foreclosure that the church could buy as a rehabilitation home for men. It had been a meth house out on the side of the foothill. Well, instead that place became our home, twenty-four years ago, and it sits on the side of a hill that I walk nearly every morning and evening. It is the place I prayed for. We all need the same thing—a place to walk alone with Jesus.

Jesus loves for us to come to Him with worship, bowing, singing, shouting, praising Him for His greatness. It is in these moments that we build intimacy with Him. It is in worship that we grow deep in our desire to have His heart in us.

Today stop and take time to look up and around you at creation—not at what man has made but at what the King has created. It is so profound that it will cause worship to rise up in you. Are you thirsty for Jesus? Do you hunger for more of Him? Do you want to be a man or woman after God's heart? Begin to build a habit of praise and adoration to the Lord, and you will begin to build a heart after God.

— PRAYER —

Father, I want to be a person who has a heart after You. I can see in the life of David that a heart after You begins in worship, so please teach me to worship You. Remind me daily that I need to stop and worship You and thank You, and that when I do, You will pour out Your presence on me. Amen.

DAY 27

....

The Sound of Worship

David spoke to the chiefs of the Levites to appoint
their relatives the singers, with instruments of music, harps, lyres,
loud-sounding cymbals, to raise sounds of joy.

1 CHRONICLES 15:16

Music is a fascinating thing. It was most certainly created by God and for God. All music leads us to worship something, because music is about worship. David, as far as we know, was the first person to link songs and music with worship. First Chronicles says that David appointed people "over the service of song in the house of the LORD, after the ark rested there" (1 Chron. 6:31) and also "the singers, with instruments of music, harps, lyres, loud-sounding cymbals, to raise sounds of joy" (1 Chron. 15:16).

We may not all be musically inclined, but we should figure this out: music is a central part of worship. I'm talking about sounds of joy that will build up our spirits and encourage us. Do you have thoughtful and worshipful music in your life? Do you play it in your car or on your phone or in your home? Far too often we fill our heads with sounds that kill, words that tear us up and bring us down, instead of bathing ourselves in worship music. No matter what kind of music we like, we can find worship music that will build us up.

Do you ever sing to the Lord? Many of us cannot carry a tune, but that is really beside the point. Singing to the Lord is part of growing into a worshiper of Him. If you hunger for intimacy with Jesus, try breaking out of your dull routine and add a bit of risk to your relationship with Him. Yes, it is risky to sing to the Lord, but it is life giving and healing. He is drawn to our hearts when we worship Him with song. Pour out your life before Him in song. Don't be ashamed. He isn't ashamed of us any more than we are of a child singing his or her heart out even when the notes are way out of tune.

Like David we must decide that we want to grow, that we want to make worshiping Jesus a focus of our lives. Start today, and be intentional about it. Get the right music in your life, and sing a new song to Him.

PRAYER

Father, may I never, ever be ashamed of worshiping You. There is no God like You, Lord. You alone can meet my needs each day, and You alone deserve my praise and adoration. I love You, Father. Teach me to worship You freely and passionately. Amen.

DAY 28

....

Worship and Thanksgiving

Enter His gates with thanksgiving and His courts with praise.
Give thanks to Him, bless His name. For the LORD is good;
His lovingkindness is everlasting and His faithfulness to all generations.

PSALM 100:4-5

The quickest way into our Father's presence is through praise. A heart set to praise the Lord is a heart open to God's healing and filling. When we are discouraged, down and depressed, thankfulness is our recipe for change, because it opens a new perspective to our situation—a hope-filled one. We begin to realize and declare that in spite of our circumstances or feelings, God is good, His loving-kindness never ends, and He will remain faithful to us even in our struggles.

Think about Thanksgiving Day—the turkey, pie, family, and friends. By the end of the day, we are full! Being thankful fills our spirits. It keeps us positioned for life in Christ. It gives us a focus we otherwise wouldn't have. Unthankful living always means unfocused faith, but thankfulness brings God's perspective to our circumstances, and it changes our attitudes toward difficult situations.

Praise and thanksgiving go together. Paul tells us that in Ephesians 5:18-20: "Be filled with the Spirit, speaking to one another in psalms and hymns and spiritual songs, singing and making melody with your heart to the Lord; always giving thanks for all things in the name of our Lord Jesus Christ to God, even the Father." He repeats the message to the Thessalonian believers: "Rejoice always; pray without ceasing; in everything give thanks; for this is God's will for you in Christ Jesus" (1 Thess. 5:16–18).

When we begin to be unthankful, we start to believe that the world owes us. Bitterness can creep in and steal our joy. It has been said that thankful people become holy people. Why is this? Because God's character is born in us when we are thankful. Our worst situations become fertile ground for His character to grow in us. Praise is released through our thankfulness that breaks the darkness, blesses God, and changes us.

The choice to praise God positions us to receive new fillings of life from the Holy Spirit, new confidence in Jesus. And thankfulness is a declaration of our trust in Jesus, a proclamation of hope beyond what we see or feel, our hope against hope in Him. Begin to practice praise and thanksgiving daily as a lifestyle, and see if Jesus doesn't enlarge your heart and hope for His purposes.

—☙ PRAYER ❧—

Jesus, birth in me a new hunger to praise You. Holy Spirit, fill my heart with thanksgiving, praise, and adoration for Jesus. Father, forgive me for grumbling. Teach me the power of being thankful—show me how it will give me life and bless Your heart. Glorify God in me and my present circumstances so that others will see Your hope in me. Thank You, Lord. Amen.

DAY 29

....

Wise Worshipers

*After Jesus was born in Bethlehem of Judea in the days of
Herod the king, magi from the east arrived in Jerusalem, saying,
"Where is He who has been born King of the Jews? For we saw
His star in the east and have come to worship Him."...
After coming into the house they saw the Child with Mary His
mother; and they fell to the ground and worshiped Him.*

MATTHEW 2:1-11

What made the wise men wise? They were worshipers. This is
the key to all right living: we must learn to worship and become worshipers of Jesus. The first and foremost commandment
is to love the Lord our God with all that we are. Jesus made this
clear in Matthew 22:37: "You shall love the Lord your God with all
your heart, and with all your soul, and with all your mind." The
wise men are a great picture of this deep, worshiping love for God.
These men traveled hundreds and hundreds of miles for one thing:
to worship Jesus. Their sacrifice was great, but that is always part
of being a worshiper.

The wise men had awaited the birth of the Savior with great
expectation. They were willing to do whatever it took, overcome
whatever obstacle they met in order to be in the presence of the
newborn Savior. They looked forward to the day with excitement
and anticipation when they would meet Him. When that moment
finally came, they were awed and overwhelmed at Jesus' presence.

They were, at last, in the presence of the King of kings and had no choice but to fall down and worship Him.

How is it that today many of us find Jesus to be average or mundane? How is it that we can come to church with little or no expectation of worshiping the Creator of the heavens and earth? Somewhere we have lost our way and misplaced the honor we are to give our King. Our first call is not to serve others but to worship God. It is out of worship for God that we are filled up, refreshed, and empowered to serve others and honor God. But worship always comes first.

Ask the Lord to renew your first love if you are having trouble worshiping Him. Remember how deep your passion for Jesus ran when you first came to Him? Hunger for that once again. It is in worship that God sets up all the rest of our destiny. Become a worshiper, bow down, and exalt your King, and He will lift you up and surpass your greatest expectations of what He can be to you.

━⟋ PRAYER ⟍━

Father, teach me the lessons of worship. I want to be like the wise men, who sacrificed all they had to come before You and worship You. Thank You for making me a person who was created to worship a God like You. Amen.

Worship from the Heart

*Araunah said to David, "Let my lord the king take and offer up
what is good in his sight. Look, the oxen for the burnt offering,
the threshing sledges and the yokes of the oxen for the wood.
Everything, O king, Araunah gives to the king."... However,
the king said to Araunah, "No, but I will surely buy it from you
for a price, for I will not offer burnt offerings to
the LORD my God which cost me nothing."*

2 SAMUEL 24:22-24

David's greatness flowed out of his worship. Even when he fell
and sinned against the Lord, he understood that the favor of
God was on his life, and he gave thanks. After his pride had driven
him to number the men in Israel in order to determine the strength
of his army and he saw his sin, David ran to the Lord, not away
from Him. He knew that the only way to heal this deep breach was
to repent and worship again.

When we fall, we can still live in the favor of God. The cross
made a way to heal our hearts and lives. We cannot redeem our
situations, but we can come to Jesus and cry out for Him to heal
us. His blood shed on Calvary is for our shortcomings, our pride,
our bad choices, our wrong thinking. Jesus died so that we can live

in spite of our sin. But we must come to Him, bow before Him, and worship Him. We must give Him our hearts, and in our surrender He will call us into deep worship with Himself.

David understood this. He likely had no idea that the place where the Lord sent him to worship was the same place where Abraham had offered his son Isaac, nor did he realize that one day the temple he hungered to build for God would be built on this very spot. What he knew was that he had to obey, and that meant taking the time to lay out his heart before the Lord and repent.

When he went to Araunah's threshing floor to worship, Araunah did what many would do for a man of David's position: he offered David all he needed to honor the Lord. But David knew that taking someone else's offering wasn't worship. This is why he said, "No, but I will surely buy it from you for a price, for I will not offer burnt offerings to the LORD my God which cost me nothing."

Worship costs us. It should take our time and energy, our heart and honesty, and in some cases, our money. When God wants something from us that is costly, it isn't because He is bankrupt; it is because He wants our hearts. David's sacrifice wasn't for God; it was for David. It bore the marks of David's heart and the message he felt deep inside. Offering ourselves to Jesus doesn't always or even often come easily, but it is always life giving and healing.

—⧼ PRAYER ⧽—

Father, today I come and lay out my life before You. Teach me to live in Your favor so that when I fail, I will run to You and not away from You. Holy Spirit, lead me into deeper worship of Jesus. I hunger to lay out my heart and life before You. Amen.

Stepping Out in Courage and Faith

*There is no way for us to measure the effect
of the risks we take to touch others' lives.
Christianity began two thousand years ago with
twelve men and some faithful followers of Jesus—
normal people who took risks and answered
the call to change the world.
Will you?*

DAY 31

....

When God Says Go

*Get your provisions ready. Three days from now you will cross
the Jordan here to go in and take possession of the land
the LORD your God is giving you for your own.*

JOSHUA 1:11, NIV

After forty years of wandering and waiting, God finally declared to Joshua in no uncertain terms, "The time is now. Go forward. God has given you a destiny, a possibility of life that you have never had, and you must get ready in three days." As we have been talking about, timing is central to all God does.

Jesus warned in Matthew 24 and 25 that no man knows the hour or the day when He will return, but it was obvious by what He said that the day and hour are established in the Father's heart. It is no different in our lives. God has our purposes established, even though we must often wait to see them fulfilled. When the time is ripe, God tells us to go forward and take the land!

While God spoke of many blessings that Israel would find in the promised land, He forgot to mention the giants! When God leads us to a promised land, it is full of great opportunities, such as a new job, a new child or friend, a new house. These things all seem to hold so much potential. But then we find that there is a catch—an unexpected cost or disappointment or challenge to face. For Israel it was giants. They faced a valley of giants in the midst of fruitful possibility—all of them ready to steal the possibility.

While lands of great opportunity always have big giants, they also have big possibilities for increasing our faith. Think for a moment of two balloons, one filled with carbon dioxide and the other with helium. The first balloon cannot rise, while the one filled with helium will immediately go up. In the same way, if our hearts are filled with doubts and fears, we will not be able to rise in faith to do what God wants us to do. But if we focus on God's promises and power and believe Him to do the impossible, we will go forward in great victory.

Will you believe beyond what you can see to become a joy to your Father, since "without faith it is impossible to please Him" (Heb. 11:6)? Go forward, even in the face of seemingly insurmountable obstacles, and trust God to give you the land.

—⌒ PRAYER ⌒—

Father, thank You that the right time for me to move is established in Your heart. Jesus, teach me to go when You say that the fruit is ripe. Holy Spirit, build faith in me that can conquer every giant in my path so that by believing in You, I will overcome them. Thank You for setting before me a land of promise. Amen.

DAY 32

....

Being Spirit Led

Those who are led by the Spirit of God are the children of God.

ROMANS 8:14, NIV

Being led by the Holy Spirit is the call of all Christians. In the book of Acts, Luke tells a story of Philip being led into the desert by an angel. He obeyed and went, and he ran into a high official of the Ethiopian government riding in a chariot and reading the book of Isaiah. Philip asked the man if he understood what he was reading, and when the man said he didn't, Philip began to explain the good news of Jesus to him. The Ethiopian then asked to be baptized that day (see Acts 8:26–39). All this for one man.

This is the work of the Spirit, one person at a time. One touch, one changed life, one destiny—His work makes walking with Jesus a great and wild adventure. When we are Spirit led, it will stretch us, but it will build and bless us at the same time. Our desires will shift from ordinary to supernatural. We will dream bigger dreams and take greater risks. God will impart divine creativity into our workplaces, our families, and our world. Our lives will reverberate with delight when He is filling and leading us.

The problem is, too often we find it easy to fall away from the Lord's direction for our lives. So many things beckon for our attention that we fail to listen for the Spirit's leading at times. We get involved in all kinds of things that don't matter—houses, cars, relationships, careers, sports, hobbies, or spending money. In the moment these things seem so important, but in the long haul, if we lose Jesus and miss His purpose for our lives, the cost is far too great. Anything that causes us to lose Him is not as important as it seemed.

How do we stay on track?

Stay in the Word. "The whole Bible was given to us by inspiration from God and is useful to teach us what is true and to make us realize what is wrong in our lives; it straightens us out and helps us do what is right" (2 Tim. 3:16, TLB).

Obey the Holy Spirit's leading. Listen for the prompting of the Holy Spirit as you read the Bible and then as you go about your day, and be ready to obey His guidance.

Walk in faith. Faith is action—we must step out in it.

Ask the Lord each day to lead and guide you, fill and anoint you, and influence all you do and say. Then you will bless His heart and minister life to those He leads you to.

—⌒ PRAYER ⌒—

Lord, You know that I often stray from Your Holy Spirit's direction. Please empower me by Your power to follow Your lead. Show me when I begin to stray, and teach me to surrender to Jesus first before all else so that I can please You and bless others. Amen.

···························

The Lord
Your Shepherd

The LORD is my shepherd, I shall not want.
He makes me lie down in green pastures;
He leads me beside quiet waters. He restores my soul.

PSALM 23:1-3

David was a remarkable man, gifted in so many ways: he was a worshiper, songwriter, king, shepherd, leader, and warrior. But of all David said and did, he is probably best remembered by the six short verses found in Psalm 23. They define him and his heart for God.

No doubt David grew into the knowledge that the Lord was his shepherd as a young boy out on a hillside with his father's flocks. It was there that he was molded and shaped by God. It was there that he led sheep and grew to understand that he actually was a sheep in the Father's flock.

But for many of us, being led by the Lord is not a joy but a struggle. We battle with yielding our wills into His hand. I have learned more about walking with Jesus through my obedient dogs than I ever have in a sermon or Bible study. When I see my dogs eager to hang with me, to please me and enjoy me, I am moved by their teachable spirit—something I long to have with my Father.

David must have felt the same way about the sheep he cared for and seen himself in that little flock.

In order for the Lord to be our shepherd, we must decide that we are happy to be one of His sheep. This is not a glamorous role, but it is a necessary one if we are to fulfill our destiny and grow in the greatness God has for us. He is our shepherd only when we humble ourselves and joyfully agree to be one of His sheep.

When we do this, life flows and takes on a new and hope-filled way. Notice, "He makes me lie down in green pastures; He leads me beside quiet waters." That may sound a little boring to us, but the green pastures and quiet waters are where we all need to go for healing and repair. David embraced the Lord's leading. "He makes me" isn't "He asks me"—it is "He leads, and I follow."

When we surrender to the Lord's leading, we get blessed: "He restores my soul." How hungry are you to have your soul restored? This is the passageway to healing and life. Open up to God's leading today. Bow down and tell Him that you hunger for His touch and yield to His leading.

⚯ PRAYER ⚭

Father, teach me to yield to You, to pour out my heart to You. Far too often I don't surrender to You and Your Spirit. Today I declare to You my heart's desire to be led by You and touched and restored by Your hand. Thank You, Father. Amen.

DAY 34

Paths of Righteousness

He guides me in the paths of righteousness for His name's sake.
Even though I walk through the valley of the shadow of death,
I fear no evil, for You are with me; Your rod and Your staff,
they comfort me. You prepare a table before me
in the presence of my enemies.

PSALM 23:3-5

Being guided by the hand of the Lord must be our daily desire. We will walk through many things this side of heaven that will blow us up. We will face difficulties—we can be sure of it. But Jesus said, "These things I have spoken to you, so that in Me you may have peace. In the world you have tribulation, but take courage; I have overcome the world" (John 16:33).

In the world we will face trials, but God has the peace and power to overcome any and every obstacle we face. David's life was after the heart of God, but it was also a life marked by pain and loss. We all need a guide in this life, a compass to keep us on track. The Lord hungers to be a shepherd leader to each of us every day. When He is leading us, He brings us into places of life and hope and healing. He leads us in paths of righteousness for His name's sake—so that His glory will shine in our lives and others will see His life and be drawn to His name.

The Lord leads us with both His rod and His staff. His rod we need when we lose our way—that is called correction. His staff nudges and encourages us to walk with Him on the narrow road. This is like a sheep with its master. When it yields to the shepherd, it finds life and relationship; when it pushes back, it finds difficulty. When we allow the Holy Spirit to correct and care for us, we find great comfort and safety, no matter what assails us.

In the midst of daily battles, God and God alone can set a table before us in the presence of our enemies. That means that we need not fear or flee; we are safe in Him. He will gird us up and guard our way. He will be a shield about us and a light for our paths.

Do we really want to be led by Him or just rescued when we get ourselves into trouble? It is here and now that our lives will be shaped and our destinies determined. Will you surrender to His will and way? No matter what life has brought your way, stop today, sit alone with God, and declare, "The LORD is my shepherd, I shall not want" (Ps. 23:1). He is your shepherd if you will yield to Him all that is bottled up inside you.

─⟋ PRAYER ⟍─

Jesus, You are the great shepherd, and You love Your sheep! Teach me to come to You daily for direction and supernatural guidance. Remind me that in the battle and grind of life, You are with me. Today I yield to Your leading, Holy Spirit, believing that You will direct my steps and correct my faults. Thank You, Lord. Amen.

DAY 35

....

Faith and Fear
Can't Live Together

The word of the LORD came to Abram in a vision, saying,
"Do not fear, Abram, I am a shield to you; your reward shall be
very great." . . . Then he believed in the LORD;
and He reckoned it to him as righteousness.

GENESIS 15:1–6

Abraham would never have been called the father of the faith
(see Rom. 4) if he had given into fear. Fear and faith can't live
together—one always overcomes the other. This doesn't mean that
we won't feel the emotion of fear; all of us do. The question is, when
we feel fear, what will we do? Where will we turn?

The Lord made a dramatic promise to Abraham here: "I am a
shield to you." This promise is given to God's people all over the
Bible: "The LORD God is a sun and shield; the LORD gives grace and
glory; no good thing does He withhold from those who walk uprightly" (Ps. 84:11), for example, and, "You are my hiding place and
my shield" (Ps. 119:114). God makes this promise to us because He
wants us to live in faith and not fear. So many people are trapped
in fear, but fear does great damage to our faith.

When the people of Israel were rebuilding the wall of Jerusalem,
enemies threatened them, and they became afraid. But Nehemiah
encouraged them: "Remember the Lord, who is great and glorious,

and fight for your brothers, your sons, your daughters, your wives, and your homes!" (Neh. 4:14, NLT).

Every move of God faces opposition from hell, including God's work in my life and yours. The forces of darkness are real and active. Only a believer who is determined to press in will break through. When you sense spiritual attack, don't freak out; stay calm, and remember how great a God you serve. Be still, and know that He is with you. Ask Him to fight the battle for you. He will.

Stay near others who love Jesus; they will build you up and help guard your life. Nehemiah spent fifty-two days rebuilding the wall around Jerusalem, a wall that had lain in ruin for years. But only by encouraging the people to press in and not give in to fear was it possible. Encouragement can go far when evil strikes. Why? When we lose our courage to fight, our desire to press in, our faith that God is in our work, encouragement like Nehemiah gave to the people reenergizes us with new courage.

The next time you are fearful, turn to God, and remember that He is your shield and your hiding place: "He Himself has said, 'I will never desert you, nor will I ever forsake you,' so that we confidently say, 'The Lord is my helper, I will not be afraid. What will man do to me?'" (Heb. 13:5-6). Don't give up the battle, and don't give in to fear. Encourage those around you to be steadfast and immovable in Jesus!

──◦ PRAYER ◦──

Jesus, I want to be a person of faith. Teach me to run to You when I feel fear. Holy Spirit, when I am fearful, remind me that I am a child of the King of kings and that there is no one I need fear. As Your Word says, "What will man do to me?" Thank You, Father, for being my shield. Amen.

DAY 36

Faith and Obedience Live Together

*By faith Abraham, when he was called, obeyed by going out
to a place which he was to receive for an inheritance;
and he went out, not knowing where he was going.*

HEBREWS 11:8

Walking with Jesus daily is sometimes difficult. It is tough to read His Word and then go out and face the world—especially when He asks us to take a stand for Him or sacrifice for Him. But without obedience our faith can never grow. Sometimes we are inclined to obey our emotions, and when they don't line up with His calling on our lives, obedience is tough. The problem with emotions is that they change from moment to moment and day to day. But God's Word and His call always remain the same.

Abraham was called the father of the faith, yet he was regularly tested by God and asked to obey. For Jesus it was no different; He was tempted by hell and pushed and pulled by people all the time. Yet He made it clear that He expected us to obey Him when He said, "If you love Me, you will keep My commandments" (John 14:15).

Obedience is easy to talk about and hard to do. It can be pretty relative, can't it? From "I gave up my craving for chocolate" to "I am selling all I own and moving to Africa." The truth is, we all learn obedience in stages. Sometimes we feel that we are all in but then realize how good we are at not actually giving everything to God but only telling ourselves we have.

What we often miss is that obedience brings blessing. We sometimes feel like having to obey is a curse, but obeying God's command takes faith, and therefore it causes our faith to grow deep. This was the story of Abraham. He was called to go, and he went, "not knowing where he was going." Wow, that is a test, isn't it? Go, but where? Just go, obey and go. F. B. Meyer said of Abraham, "Where he went, he knew not; it was enough to know he went with God. He leaned not so much upon the promises as upon the Promisor. He looked not on the difficulties of his situation, but on his King."[1] Thankfully, when Jesus asks us to obey, He is often clear about His directions. But even when He is not, surrendering to Him and His will is our best and only life-giving option.

The journey is one of faith, not sight, so there will be times when it is hard for us to see what God is up to. But that is the faith part: obey, and watch Him work; disobey, and we miss the blessing of growing in our faith in Him.

⌇ PRAYER ⌇

Jesus, teach me to obey, not kicking and screaming, but surrendering to You and joyfully anticipating what it is You are about to do. I want to live a faith-filled life, and I realize that this can happen only when I obey. Holy Spirit, empower me to obey, and give me a hunger to obey and a joy when I do obey. Thank You, Father, that Your way works. Amen.

DAY 37

Getting Beyond Your Fears

Be strong and courageous, because you will lead these people to inherit the land I swore to their ancestors to give them. Be strong and very courageous.

JOSHUA 1:6, NIV

Any time we talk about surrendering to God, our greatest struggle is usually fear. So many fears creep into our thoughts: *What will He want from me? I know that I will fail Him.* There is good news here: Jesus is the God of second and third and sixty-third chances! You will fail, and so will I, but God never does. Don't give in to fear; it will rob you of life every time.

After the people of Israel failed to believe that God would bring them into the promised land, they wandered around a desert for forty years until all those who had been afraid to believe God were gone. The new generation, led by Joshua, had the opportunity to once again face the giants of their fathers. Because as we have seen, one thing is true: we will have giants to face.

We never outgrow our feelings of fear, but rather we must learn to overcome them. As people who are positioned in Christ, we can receive a tremendous amount of courage by the faith God has given us: "Everyone born of God overcomes the world. This is the victory that has overcome the world, even our faith" (1 John 5:4, NIV). It isn't so much that we will ever lose our fear of the giants in our lives, but rather we will grow to understand that by the faith God gives every believer, we will overcome them.

You see, just before God commanded Joshua to be strong and courageous, He gave him a promise: "Every place on which the sole of your foot treads, I have given it to you" (Josh. 1:3). This is a staggering thought, because it means that we are to *believe before we see*. Can you see the promise fulfilled before it comes about? J. Oswald Sanders, who oversaw Overseas Missionary Fellowship, said, "Eyes that look are common. Eyes that see are rare." This type of faith is life giving, because a faith that believes to see holds back discouragement.

What fears do you have today that need to be overcome? Are you willing to trust in an invisible God, even when you don't feel like it? Joshua and the children of Israel faced their giants, by faith doing what God had instructed them to do, and by that demonstration of faith, the people were victorious.

─◌ PRAYER ◌─

Father, give me a faith to overcome, a faith that will no longer be held captive by fear but will conquer fear. Teach me to see with eyes in my heart that look beyond the natural—to believe with a faith that will not only liberate me but also heal others and set them free as You work through me. Thank You for the truth that we are victorious in Christ Jesus. Amen.

DAY 38

You Are Not a Grasshopper in God's Eyes

We even saw giants there, the descendants of Anak.
Next to them we felt like grasshoppers, and that's what they thought, too!

NUMBERS 13:33, NLT

What an interesting verse: "We felt like grasshoppers, and they thought the same thing!" Our perceptions can certainly get us into trouble fast, can't they? There were giants in the land, but that is no reason for us to feel like grasshoppers! When we lose perspective, we lose faith, and when we lose faith, we have lost relationship with Jesus.

When confronted with giants, how do you respond? For those who are cowards at heart, the first response is generally to flee. God had led His chosen people to the promised land. But the reports of giants living in the land struck fear into their hearts and caused them to doubt God's promises. Only Caleb and Joshua trusted God for their deliverance and inheritance. To them these giants were little more than a challenge to be overcome by trusting in a faithful God.

God seems to put His people into situations that are regularly way over our heads. He often calls us to invest ourselves into something bigger than we are, something beyond our natural abilities and capabilities. But He asks us to give to the work of His kingdom and then believe that He will give us supernatural gifts and talents to accomplish His work.

I used to doubt that He could do that with me, and I am sure many of you feel the same. But my journey has convinced me He will use anybody who makes themselves available. Release your fears to God; you are not adequate for His work, but He is! Paul put it this way: "Not that we are sufficient of ourselves to claim anything as coming from us, but our sufficiency is from God, who has made us sufficient to be ministers of a new covenant" (2 Cor. 3:5-6, ESV).

Most of the time the giants in our lives are not as big as we suspect they might be. But again, our perception is often huge and inaccurate. I think Jim Elliot rightly said it when he wrote, "The shadow a thing casts often far exceeds the size of the thing itself." Today these "descendants of Anak" take on the form of broken families, rebellious children, an impossible boss, cancer. They can look imposing and so big when we first confront them. But don't lose perspective. We serve a great God who is *huge*.

When facing giants in our lives, we have but two responses: either we believe that we can overcome the giants, or we believe that the giants will overcome us. Which is it for you? Do you view yourself as a grasshopper or a giant killer? Trust in a faithful God, and be fearless in the presence of giants.

—☙ PRAYER ❧—

Dear Lord, make me a courageous Christian. Teach me to live by faith, not by sight. Make me a believer who will be willing to fight any giant that may come across my path, not in my own strength, but in Yours as You supply it by Your Holy Spirit. Amen.

DAY 39

....

Facing Your Giants

*Saul said to David, "You are not able to go against
this Philistine to fight with him; for you are but a youth
while he has been a warrior from his youth."*

1 SAMUEL 17:33

David and Goliath—those two names are forever tied together. David had slowly grown over the years into a deeper and deeper love relationship with the Lord. It was in solitude that David had been shaped into the giant slayer he became. We never become this strong overnight, so it is vital to remember that waiting with God is never a waste of time—it is part of the journey. David's courage and faith were born during his seasons alone with God, and without them he would have never been able to face the giant!

We too have giants in our lives. They may take the shape of a person who makes us miserable or a job we hate, a friend or loved one we've lost or a sickness or injury we cannot shake. Giants are part of life. Yes, they are often scary, but they are a part of our lives, and we must all face them.

There will also always be men like Saul around to discourage us rather than encourage us. If David had listened to Saul in those moments before he faced Goliath, he would have missed his destiny. But he listened to the Spirit of God instead, and that is where his victory was born. Who do we listen to? We all have people who discourage us. But we need to be intentional about getting into places where Spirit-filled believers can encourage us—a small group, the School of Ministry, a ministry to serve in, or a place where we can give life to others. It is when we fellowship with His people that the Holy Spirit will impart courage to us to move ahead with Him.

All of us need others to encourage us, or, as the word "encourage" literally means, impart courage in us. Ask the Holy Spirit to both encourage you and make you an encourager today. Prayerfully make it a point to encourage those around you, knowing that many of them are facing their own giants, even though they may never let on that they are.

PRAYER

Lord, forgive me for all the times I have discouraged others, many of them facing giants that I had no idea about. Holy Spirit, impart encouragement to me today so that I will have a river of life flowing out of me that will encourage others. Amen.

DAY 40

....

Your Battle Is Not with Flesh and Blood

Our struggle is not against flesh and blood, but against the rulers,
against the powers, against the world forces of this darkness,
against the spiritual forces of wickedness in the heavenly places.
Therefore, take up the full armor of God, so that you will be able
to resist in the evil day, and having done everything, to stand firm.

EPHESIANS 6:12-13

David's battle with Goliath was a clear Old Testament picture of spiritual warfare. Goliath's people, the Philistines, often portrayed the darkness of Satan to the people of God. They were a shadow of a far deeper reality. Paul speaks of that reality in Ephesians 6:12, telling us that we are in a battle every day—not with those around us but with unseen powers and principalities who form the forces of darkness and wickedness. For some of us, the thought of the battle sends shivers down our spine. We are terrified at the very thought of a spirit realm with real demonic forces that can battle us and, God forbid, that we might have to face! Many of us are petrified at the thought.

But we are not alone in the battle! First John 4:4 reminds us, "Greater is He who is in you than he who is in the world." We need to wake up to our reality. Life is a battle, and Jesus is the victor! He wins, and we are in Him, so we win! We must not allow darkness to overshadow His life and light in us. The Lord has imparted spiritual authority to His children, so there is no reason for us to cower in fear, no reason to shrink back from the battle. If we are His, then hell knows we are a danger and a deep threat. Take courage—Jesus in us is far more than Satan wants to tackle.

Bow down and worship Jesus today. Cry out to Him, and ask for Him to put a hedge around you. Then, as Paul tells us, "Take up the full armor of God, so that you will be able to resist in the evil day, and having done everything, to stand firm."

Be encouraged; stand firm; don't give in. God can enable you to do it as you yield to Him. Don't strike out at others. Act in the spirit opposite that of darkness, and God's light will overcome the evil. Invite God's Spirit to abide in you and empower you. He will. Then stand and watch Him take what the enemy meant for evil and turn it to good. This is what spiritual warfare is about: thwarting the intent and strategies of Satan and turning them into blessings. This may sound impossible in your situation, but nothing is impossible with God. Trust in Him, and He will give you victory.

—⁊ PRAYER ⁊—

Father, it seems that every day the battle is on. People hassle me and make me miserable inside and out. Would You, Holy Spirit, touch me with Your power and bring a love to my heart that I am often missing in the battle—a love that will break darkness and release Your light? Amen.

Don't Allow Fear to Rule You

David came to Nob to Ahimelech the priest; and Ahimelech came trembling to meet David and said to him, "Why are you alone and no one with you?" David said to Ahimelech the priest, "The king has commissioned me with a matter and has said to me, 'Let no one know anything about the matter on which I am sending you and with which I have commissioned you; and I have directed the young men to a certain place.'"

1 SAMUEL 21:1-2

Many emotions drive us, but none is as debilitating as fear. Certainly fear can be life saving in the right circumstances, but so often we are afraid when we have no need to be. Fear tells us to back away from risk taking, and risk taking is a daily part of faith living.

On the surface it appears that the priest, Ahimelech, was the one frozen with fear, but a closer look brings reality into focus. Ahimelech was reading the situation correctly. The king would never have sent David on a mission without a large contingent of soldiers. The truth is, David was running from Saul for his life. The person ruled by fear was David, not the priest. David, the one who had lived in great faith and slain the giant, had given in to fear.

We all have moments when fear paralyzes us. We all have weaknesses and situations that break us. David did as well. Here he was lying through his teeth because he was afraid. His fear had gripped him and driven him to deception. Fear kills faith, and when we embrace fear, we can be certain that we are losing faith. That is exactly what happened to David during this period of time.

King Saul had thrown spears at David in the royal palace and made it clear that if he could, he would kill David, so certainly David's fear was not without some merit. But what about the promises of God? Samuel had anointed David king, and God had promised His covering over David, yet like many of us, he was overwhelmed with fear.

When fear attacks us, our greatest assets are the promises of God. The Bible is literally packed full of promises that can arrest our fears. Find them, meditate on them, and believe them. God will never abandon you or forsake you. Jesus is deeply in love with you. Begin today with this great promise: "'I know the plans that I have for you,' declares the LORD, 'plans for welfare and not for calamity to give you a future and a hope. Then you will call upon Me and come and pray to Me, and I will listen to you. You will seek Me and find Me when you search for Me with all your heart'" (Jer. 29:11-13).

—⌒ PRAYER ⌒—

Lord, I can see that my fears keep me from experiencing Your hope and life. Teach me to meditate on Your promises, spend time in Your Word, and believe You so that I can live in faith each day. Thank You, Father, that Your love for me is deep and wide. Remind me of that each time fear begins to threaten my heart. Amen.

DAY 42

....

Believe and Engage

Every place on which the sole of your foot treads,
I have given it to you.

JOSHUA 1:3

It is tough to live by faith. It is hard to believe in what we cannot see, but that is what a faith walk is about—surrendering to a living God who asks us to rely on Him. That is really what Joshua 1:3 is about—get up and believe, walk the land, and engage. I know that we cannot see anything happening when we walk, but our participation is crucial for the final outcome to be victorious.

The writer of Hebrews tells us that "faith is confidence in what we hope for and assurance about what we do not see" (Heb. 11:1, NIV). This type of faith is life giving. It builds hope and holds off discouragement. It engages with God even when it cannot see the outcome. It wins the battles in life because it believes that if God is for us, who can stand against us?

The land God had promised the Israelites covered a ton of territory, but most of it was never possessed, because Israel gave up. They quit believing and obeying. Don't give up! In January 1993, the Buffalo Bills in the NFL pulled off one of the greatest comebacks of all time. They trailed thirty-five to three in the third quarter, and it appeared the Houston Oilers had an insurmountable lead, so the fans gave up and started leaving. But the Bills mounted a comeback for the ages that day and pulled the game out forty-one to thirty-eight. The only problem was, a bunch of people missed it!

After Jesus was crucified, two of His followers gave up. They left town and started walking to Emmaus. They had heard the report that He had risen from the dead, but they didn't believe it. Jesus met them on that road and showed them they were in the middle of the greatest miracle comeback ever seen, and they didn't know it. Galatians 6:9 tells us, "Let's not get tired of doing what is good. At just the right time we will reap a harvest of blessing if we don't give up" (NLT).

Fear imprisons; faith liberates. Fear paralyzes; faith empowers. Fear disheartens; faith encourages. Fear sickens; faith heals. Fear makes useless; faith makes serviceable. And, most of all, fear puts hopelessness at the heart of life, while faith rejoices in its God. We can't see all that God is up to, but we can walk the land and believe that He has already given us the victory. Obey what Jesus is asking you to do today, and let Him worry about tomorrow.

PRAYER

Lord, teach me to see with eyes of the heart that look beyond the natural. Help me believe with a faith that will liberate not only me but others as well. Holy Spirit, give me a faith that helps others become healed and set free as You work through me. Thank You, Father. Amen.

DAY 43

....

Faith Versus Fear

Caleb silenced the people before Moses and said,
"We should go up and take possession of the land, for we can certainly
do it." But the men who had gone up with him said,
"We can't attack those people; they are stronger than we are."

NUMBERS 13:30–31, NIV

Caleb was a remarkable man. At age forty he went into the promised land as one of the twelve spies. Only he and Joshua remained faithful to what the Lord had spoken to Israel, even as the other ten spies injected fear and unbelief into the people. We hear very little about Caleb, but all we do hear is good. We are told that Caleb had "a different spirit" and followed the Lord fully (Num. 14:24). Wow, what a description.

Because Caleb followed the Lord faithfully, Moses promised him land as an inheritance. But do you know what land he was promised? A land filled with giants! Caleb's attitude regarding this came from his heart, which always remained true: "Now then, give me this hill country about which the LORD spoke on that day, for you heard on that day that Anakim [giants] were there, with great fortified cities; perhaps the LORD will be with me, and I will drive them out as the LORD has spoken" (Josh. 14:12).

The devotional *Streams in the Desert* puts it like this:

If we have the faith that believes to see, it will keep us from growing discouraged. We shall "laugh at impossibilities," we shall watch with delight to see how God is going to open up a path through the Red Sea, when there is no human way out of our difficulty. It is just in such places of severe testing that our faith grows and strengthens.[2]

Caleb had an attitude of abundance. He believed beyond what he could see. Caleb and Joshua were the only two of all the thousands of people in Israel who did this. Too many of us turn away from possibility instead of into it. Solomon was said to be the wisest man in the world, but when he wrote the book of Ecclesiastes, he said, "As I looked at everything I had worked so hard to accomplish, it was all so meaningless—like chasing the wind. There was nothing really worthwhile anywhere" (Eccles. 2:11, NLT). When we live apart from God, we can end up feeling the futility that Solomon expressed here. Jesus said, "Apart from Me you can do nothing" (John 15:5). But when we live in trusting obedience to Jesus, we come alive.

Bill Hybels, pastor of Willow Creek Community Church, asks, "What would it feel like to lay your head on your pillow at night and say, 'You know what I did today? I teamed up with God to change the world'?"[3] Caleb saw with faith. He was not discouraged by giants—he laughed at the seeming impossibility they presented. Others allowed fear to destroy their faith. God is inviting you to join Him on the mission of changing the world. Don't miss Him today.

—◌ PRAYER ◌—

Lord, help me trust You as I face the impossible. I love You. You offer me the same protection Caleb had: a constant reminder of Your presence that teaches me that You will always be there to protect and lead me. Thank You, Father. Amen.

DAY 44

Being a Risk Taker

It seemed good to us, having become of one mind,
to select men to send to you with our beloved Barnabas and Paul,
men who have risked their lives for the name of
our Lord Jesus Christ.

ACTS 15:25–26

Many of us live our lives close to the vest, so to speak. We are always leery of a risk. But faith is just that, a risk, and when we learn to surrender to Jesus, we figure out that He will ask us to take risks. The men in these verses were men who risked their lives for Jesus' name. That is part of living by faith—taking risks for Jesus.

God will ask us to take risks on people, people with bad reputations who need us to help them get whole. Barnabas did just that for a zealous ex-Pharisee named Saul. He took him under his wing and discipled him. He poured his life into him when he had nothing to gain and everything to lose. Jesus did that when He forgave a demonized lady named Mary Magdalene and allowed her to become one of His followers. Abraham risked his life to rescue his nephew Lot from the kings who had conquered their land, and this after Lot had taken advantage of his uncle's favor and taken the best of his land.

You have probably never heard of Edward Kimble. He was a Sunday school teacher who one day felt compelled to take a risk and share his faith with a young shoe salesman named Dwight L.

Moody. That day Moody accepted Christ and went on to become one of his generation's greatest evangelists.

Years later a man named F. B. Meyer heard him preach, and it changed his destiny and set him to begin his own evangelistic ministry. One day Wilbur Chapman, a college student, heard Meyer preach, and he too accepted Christ. Wilbur Chapman ended up impacting a baseball player named Billy Sunday, who later began his own preaching ministry.

In 1924 at a Billy Sunday crusade in Charlotte, North Carolina, hundreds of people gave their hearts to Jesus. This moved some of the businessmen in town to have another crusade with a man named Mordecai Hamm preaching. Not many were saved, but on one of the last nights, a young man named Billy Graham came down the aisle to receive Jesus. That man has preached to more than 210 million people in more than 185 countries and territories.

There is no way for us to measure and fully know the effect of the risks we take to touch others' lives. Christianity began two thousand years ago with twelve men and some faithful followers of Jesus. The rest is, as we say, history. Normal people who took risks and answered the call each day changed the world. Will you?

—⊙ PRAYER ⊙—

Father, I am not by nature a risk taker. I often pull back from taking risks. Teach me, Holy Spirit, how and when to take the risks You want me to take. I desire to grow in You, and I understand that growing in faith requires stepping out in faith. Help me trust You to meet me in the risk. Thank You, Father. Amen.

DAY 45

....

Possessing
God's Promises

Surely the LORD has given all the land into our hands.

JOSHUA 2:24

The book of Joshua teaches us principles for possessing God's promises and living out our potential. God's promises are for us to possess, and Joshua tells us how we can take the promises of God and live in them. It tells the story of a people, Israel, who moved out of slavery but struggled to move into the fullness of victory.

Many of us are stuck in the same battle. It is one thing to be a freed slave but quite another to be a person of promise—to conquer the land, to help and heal other people. It is one thing as a young Christian to have God feed us daily with "manna" by giving us what we need. It is quite another for us to sow and reap daily by deliberately investing into the kingdom of God. Both are miraculous, but manna is handed to us as young believers, and the produce of the promised land comes as we partner with God to receive. As we grow in Jesus, He expects more and more from us. He wants us to press into places we have feared to go before. He wants us to believe for others' lives and destinies.

Joshua's life was marked out by God to change others. So were Nehemiah's and those of so many others named in the Word. The truth is, we are all marked out by God for a destiny that will touch others' lives, and that destiny can change a situation for generations to come. One defining moment that still impacts America was when Dr. Martin Luther King Jr. gave a speech entitled "I Have a Dream." His words inspired a generation of people to participate in a cause bigger than they were. It was one voice that moved many hearts and mobilized people to change a nation.

God is still creating moments for us to touch poor, voiceless people who have cried out to Him for help. He will use you and me to do just that if we will prayerfully respond to the challenge and consider how we can make a difference in our generation. We have great possibilities to possess as the people of God. Possibilities of serving the poor, loving children, healing the wounded, teaching the Word, and taking the story of salvation to people all around the world. But this will take a willingness to possess the promises of God and move into the victory God has for us.

Grow deep in your relationships with the Lord and possess all He has for you. Don't be willing to live with less than all He intends for you.

PRAYER

Father, create in me a passionate desire to have all that You desire for my life. Help me not to be satisfied with anything less. Father, I desire to be more than a slave set free. Make me a person of promise, one who will be a light in darkness and a giver of hope to the hopeless. Thank You, Lord. Amen.

DAY 46

Life Is a Battle

All your fighting men, ready for battle, must cross over ahead of your
fellow Israelites. You are to help them until the LORD gives them rest,
as he has done for you, and until they too have taken possession of
the land the LORD your God is giving them.

JOSHUA 1:14-15

God's sovereignty doesn't preclude human responsibility.
Promise and blessing rarely just tumble into our hands—we
have to go after them. After Joshua crossed over the Jordan River,
the battle for the promised land had only begun. The next twenty
years of his life would be spent fighting God's battles, and he was
eighty years old!

The first eleven chapters of Joshua are about battles that had
to be fought. Joshua's life was one battle after another, yet he never
gave up. Maybe you can relate deeply to this kind of living. While
you watch others who seem to have carefree lives, that is not your
reality. Life seems to come at you in waves, and it is hard just to
keep your head above water. You wonder, *Could God really be in any*
of this? The answer is found here in Joshua. Yes, He can and often is
in the middle of these life-altering battles.

These battles can be very wearying, and discouragement can
quickly become a greater enemy than the one we were fighting. But
it is vital for us to remember that when we partner with God, no
enemy we face will be able to stand: "No man will be able to stand

before you all the days of your life. . . . I will be with you; I will not fail you or forsake you" (Josh. 1:5).

In September 1776, a young American patriot named Nathan Hale was captured by the British as a spy behind enemy lines and sentenced to death by execution. The loss of this one young man may have gone unnoticed during this war had he not said something so profound that it moved the entire American army to greater sacrifice. He said, "I only regret that I have but one life to lose for my country." God is looking for people who will surrender fully to Him in the midst of the battles we face and lay down their lives for Him. Such sacrifice and courage can make a difference in eternity.

The future always holds both blessing and battles. You can make a difference if you continue to serve God in the midst of your battles and entrust your life to Him.

PRAYER

Lord, please strengthen me with Your Holy Spirit. Renew me as I press on for You. Remind me that You are the One who fights and that I am the one who trusts and prays. Amen.

DAY 47

An Attitude of Abundance

The people who live in the land are strong, and the cities are fortified and very large; and moreover, we saw the descendants of Anak there. . . .
Why is the LORD bringing us into this land, to fall by the sword?
Our wives and our little ones will become plunder;
would it not be better for us to return to Egypt?

NUMBERS 13:28; 14:3

Sometimes the circumstances before us seem overwhelming. We look at them and are cast down. "How could God do this to me?" we ask. It appears that He has set us up for failure. Joshua was told that he would take the land, but he was also told that the "cities were fortified," ready for battle. This is often the case for us. God sets before us a land of promise, but it is also a land of battle. But we should not allow this to cast our hearts down. God is with us every step of the way. We must keep our hearts and spirits right.

It is easy to have a poverty mentality when things don't go our way—a small-mindedness about our possibilities in Christ. This attitude of poverty kills God's promises and possibilities in us. Life can be rough—we've all experienced it—but how we respond to life's bumps will depend on whether we believe that God is for us or against us. Even the widow with her mite believed that God was bigger than her circumstances (see Mark 12:41-44). Andrew

Murray spoke to this: "The power to believe a promise depends entirely on faith in the promiser."[4] If we trust in a person, then we will trust in that person's word. When we know the true, good, and loving nature of the Promiser, then we will have faith in what He promises.

Each day I try to remind myself, "You are either growing closer or moving further away from God." When I remember that, it helps me press into Him. It causes me to believe that each day has value with Him. If we invite the Holy Spirit in and tell Him we are eager to grow, He will search and purify and build us. Fear, on the other hand, drives us away from God. We don't have to let fear dictate our destinies.

Do you live paralyzed in fear or emboldened with faith? Do you have an attitude of abundance or of poverty? Having an attitude of abundance is a choice of the will. Will you choose today to trust Him?

─៚ PRAYER ៚─

Thank You, Lord, for always being for me and supplying all my needs in Christ! Create in me an attitude of abundance that will cause me to believe beyond what I can see. I know that You will do it. Amen.

DAY 48

....

When Life Gets Dark, Don't Give Up

David departed from there and escaped to the cave of Adullam;
and when his brothers and all his father's household heard of it,
they went down there to him.

1 SAMUEL 22:1

This time in David's life was painfully difficult. He was on the run from King Saul, who was crazy with envy and fear. The only place David could find refuge was in a cave in the desert. This seems on the surface so wrong and so unjust. Yet David landing in that cave was perfect for what God needed to do to make him the greatest king Israel would ever have. Caves can do that for us. Good things can happen in dark and lonely places. David was lonely and rejected, yet he pressed in to God.

David had been anointed king but was now living in a cave. This is not unlike our Savior. He too was anointed King while not yet fully ruling, while another unworthy of the throne ruled over the land. The only kingdom David had was in a cave, but it was perfect for the work our Father had to do in him. Paul writes of how what God values is often very different from what we consider best:

Consider your calling, brethren, that there were not many wise according to the flesh, not many mighty, not many noble; but God has chosen the foolish things of the world to shame the wise, and God has chosen the weak things of the world to shame the things which are strong, and the base things of the world and the despised God has chosen, the things that are not, so that He may nullify the things that are. (1 Cor. 1:26–29)

The caves David hid in can still be seen in the desert of Israel. When I once visited there, I was struck by the quiet peaceful sense of the place, a place where God could talk and a person could listen. It was here that David's heart grew deep in relationship with his Father. Listen to the words he wrote while in this cave: "Save me, O God, by your name, and vindicate me by your power. Hear my prayer, O God; give ear to the words of my mouth. . . . Behold, God is my helper; the Lord is the sustainer of my soul" (Ps. 54:1–4).

God is our helper. The Lord is the sustainer of our souls. Say that aloud, would you? Listen to those words. Make a declaration today that no matter what you are up against, your trust will be in your helper, your God. By His great power He can help you, no matter what or who is attacking you.

——— PRAYER ———

Jesus, You are incredible. Your ways are certainly not my ways, but they work to build Your heart in me. Please remind me of that when I am in the battle and lonely and feel locked away in a cave. Thank You, Lord. Amen.

DAY 49

....

When Things Make No Sense

Everyone who was in distress, and everyone who was in debt,
and everyone who was discontented gathered to him; and he became
captain over them. Now there were about four hundred men with him.

1 SAMUEL 22:2

Often we miss the things God is doing in us. We overlook them or underestimate them. Because they are spiritual and supernatural, they make no sense to our human minds and emotions. If we take what God was doing with David in the cave of Adullam, it appears to be almost ridiculous. A young man anointed king but living in a cave attracted an army of ragtag men who had failed in life and were pretty unhappy people. Those who were in distress, discontent, and in debt are the ones the Lord trusted to David to change his world.

Stop and think about it. Isn't this what Jesus does? He gathers the bruised, the poor, and the outcast—those whose lives are broken—to build His kingdom. Jesus called them the weary and heavily weighed down: "Come to Me, all who are weary and heavy-laden, and I will give you rest" (Matt. 11:28). David knew them because they came to him looking for a second chance. These were the people God used to mold and shape David—not the best and the brightest but the broken and discontent.

Is this you today, broken and discontent? Does your life seem upside down and empty? Don't give up! Give in to Jesus. He is crazy about you in spite of all your issues. He can take you and turn your mess into a destiny. That is exactly what He did with David and this motley band of broken guys.

God may take you to a cave, a dark place, to rebuild you and renew His hand in your life. Don't think that this indicates failure. On the contrary, it very well may mean that you, like David, are positioned for a new and grand move of God. Bow your heart down today and call out to your King, as David did in Psalm 57:1-3:

> Be gracious to me, O God, be gracious to me, for my soul takes refuge in You; and in the shadow of your wings I will take refuge until destruction passes by. I will cry to God Most High, to God who accomplishes all things for me. He will send from heaven and save me; He reproaches him who tramples upon me. God will send forth His lovingkindness and His truth.

It was in this cave that David pressed back in to God. It was in this cave that his humility and faith were reborn. It was in this cave that his worship began to rise up new and fresh, and it was in this cave that David's heart began to be filled with thanksgiving once again. It is often like that in caves—God gets back on the throne of our lives, where He belongs.

—◌ PRAYER ◌—

Today, Father, life feels dark, and I feel defeated. Pick me up, please, and remind me that in You I can never really lose. Teach me, Holy Spirit, to trust You when I have no idea what You are doing in me. Thank You, Lord, for never leaving me or forsaking me. Amen.

DAY 50

God Wants to Show You Favor

Joseph's master took him and put him into the jail, the place where the king's prisoners were confined; and he was there in the jail. But the LORD was with Joseph and extended kindness to him, and gave him favor in the sight of the chief jailer.

GENESIS 39:20-21

We find two important lessons in Genesis 39:20-21. The first is that even though Joseph did the right thing and received a wrong outcome, he didn't let it sour his heart. Have you ever obeyed the Lord and then—*wham!*—you got fired or someone lied about you? How did you handle it? Our response is crucial to our destiny. C. S. Lewis, in his book *The Problem of Pain*, writes, "God whispers in our pleasures, speaks in our conscience, but shouts in our pain."[5] A soft, trusting response to pain positions us for God's favor on our lives. A resentful, angry, bitter heart removes possibility for us. God wants us in a place where He can favor us.

The second lesson is that sometimes we can't make a way for ourselves—only God can forge a path for us. Earning our way is part of life for many of us; working hard and pushing through come naturally for those who are successful. Joseph was a sharp, successful guy, thoughtful and resourceful and talented and with many gifts, but he was thrown to the bottom of circumstances over

111

and over. But he always rose to the top. Why? Not because he made his own way but because he depended on the Lord to make a way for him. That didn't mean he didn't engage and work hard—he did. But he also put his trust in the Lord, not in himself.

Both of these lessons show us that God wants to favor His people. Wow, what a thought. People who grow in Christ have to figure this out; He gives us what we don't deserve and cannot earn. He sees us in ways we have never seen ourselves. He sees us as blessed, chosen, adopted, accepted, redeemed, forgiven, and positioned for greatness in Him.

This is what urges us on to do as Paul said in Ephesians 4:1: "Live a life worthy of the calling you have received" (NIV). When we believe God and allow His Spirit to instruct and correct us, when we ask Him to show us how He sees us, we begin to see His favor all over our journeys.

Many of you do not believe that God wants to favor you, but He does. Stop today and ask Him to help you keep a tender heart toward Him and let Him make a way for you. It will change your day—and your destiny.

⁓ PRAYER ⁓

Jesus, when things don't go my way, remind me to stay in, not to give up or allow bitterness to permeate me. I want Your will and Your way, and I need Your favor in my world. Teach me to remain strong if I am wronged, not to give up or give in to wrong attitudes. Thank You that as I trust You and walk with You, I will be surprised by Your favor in my circumstances. Amen.

DAY 51

Trust God to Come Through

Nothing will be impossible with God.

LUKE 1:37

God specializes in the miraculous. What we can't do, He can. What is crazy and impossible to us is completely possible with Him. What a monumental promise this is: "Nothing will be impossible with God"!

Like God, each of us loves to see the impossible done. Yet we stumble in our faith. Take heart! Mary did too. She asked the angel, "How can this be, since I am a virgin?" (Luke 1:34). But the angel spoke the promise, "The Holy Spirit will come upon you, and the power of the Most High will overshadow you" (Luke 1:35)— a promise to Mary certainly, but also to each of us. As we invite the Holy Spirit to work in us, we, like Mary, become positioned for the miraculous.

Often we are called by God to do things that we don't necessarily understand or comprehend. Many times we don't feel like doing what He asks. It may seem to be inconvenient or at the wrong time. We may not have the resources or the knowledge as to how to do something. But God is looking for obedient hearts that will simply trust Him and do what He asks.

Andrew Murray wrote, "While faith is the simplest exercise of the spiritual life, it is also the highest."[6] Faith may be the simplest and highest exercise of the spiritual life, but it is not the easiest. It is hard to trust when we can't see. Ask anyone who has played the game of being blindfolded and asked to fall backward while trusting another person to catch him or her. Few have the ability to extend faith where they can't see, but that is exactly what God wants from us: "Faith is confidence in what we hope for and assurance about what we do not see" (Heb. 11:1, NIV).

Moses modeled this for us: "By faith he left Egypt, not fearing the King's anger; he persevered because he saw him who is invisible" (Heb. 11:27, NIV). Moses obeyed God because he was able to see beyond the circumstance to the reality of Christ and the promise. Are you willing to trust in the invisible God, even when you don't feel like it? If so, you have obtained to the highest!

Don't surrender to despair and unbelief. Believe that God can do what we simply cannot. He loves us and is crazy about us and our journey with Him. He doesn't want to hurt us but to build us into His image and touch us with His glory.

Take heart. God is looking for a Holy Spirit-surrendered faith—a faith that He alone can make miraculous and victorious. Give Him His proper place today as Lord over all your circumstances, and you will be surprised as He births a miracle in you.

⟶ PRAYER ⟵

Holy Spirit, today I surrender to Your miraculous ways. Teach me to trust You even when I don't see You. Please fill me with Your presence, and build in me a victorious faith that will bring glory to Jesus and blessings to Your heart. Amen.

DAY 52

....

Gain Courage
from Jesus

Have I not commanded you? Be strong and courageous! Do not tremble or be dismayed, for the LORD your God is with you wherever you go.

JOSHUA 1:9

In the midst of any undertaking for the Lord, fear and discouragement can be two of a Christian's worst enemies. Faith is action; we must step out in it. But fear and discouragement can keep us paralyzed. What is courage? Not the absence of fear but the willingness to move ahead in spite of it. Winston Churchill is reported to have said, "Success is never final; failure is never fatal. It is courage that counts." Paul wrote to encourage the believers in Corinth, "Be on your guard; stand firm in the faith; be courageous; be strong" (1 Cor. 16:13, NIV).

Vision and change can only be implemented by people of courage. Joshua was a wise leader (see Deut. 34:9) but still a leader in need of courage. Three times in Joshua 1 God spoke to Joshua, "Be strong and courageous." The root word for "courageous" actually means to harden the will, to allow steel to grow in the heart. It does not mean to harden the heart with false pretense or sin but to be certain of what God is doing and ready to stay in it, no matter what. God was telling Joshua to harden his will in order to lay hold of all that had been set before him.

115

As our faith grows, we see throughout Scripture that courage must grow with it. God has promised to meet us with the power and possibility we need if we will spend time with Him. Isaiah 40:29–31 tells us this: "He gives strength to the weary, and to him who lacks might He increases power. Though youths grow weary and tired, and vigorous young men stumble badly, yet those who wait for the LORD will gain new strength." To accomplish any great thing for the kingdom of God takes reliance on Him. This requires time with Him, which develops a deepening relationship with Him.

How we spend our time reveals what we value. If we spend time building relationship with Jesus, it indicates how dependent we are on the Holy Spirit to move in and through us. If we don't, we are saying to God, "I can fly on my own; I don't really need relationship with You." Dependence on Jesus produces both power and courage in us.

If we are going to accomplish anything eternal this side of heaven, it will take courage—courage that we can only get through time with Jesus. Are you afraid to step out in faith? Spend more time with Jesus; He is the "author and perfecter of faith" (Heb. 12:2). Steel your will, and take hold of all that God has set before you!

—◌ PRAYER ◌—

Father, make me a person of courage, willing to trust You and take risks. Teach me to press through in prayer and take the land You have set before me. Teach me, Holy Spirit, to allow You to put Your hand on my heart so that I can move ahead with faith, not fear. Thank You, Jesus. Amen.

DAY 53

A Great Fall

When evening came David arose from his bed and walked around on
the roof of the king's house, and from the roof he saw a woman bathing;
and the woman was very beautiful in appearance.... David sent
messengers and took her, and when she came to him, he lay with her....
The woman conceived; and she sent and told David, and said,
"I am pregnant."

2 SAMUEL 11:2–5

Looking seems so innocent, yet it can get us into so much trouble. Our eyes can be our downfall, for they open the gate to our hearts. First John 2:16 says, "The world offers only a craving for physical pleasure, a craving for everything we see, and pride in our achievements and possessions. These are not from the Father, but are from this world" (NLT).

This craving for everything we see can make life so difficult. David was now the king over all Israel. He had the power to take what he saw, and when he saw this beautiful woman, he did. It is such an easy thing for any of us, when we have position or power, to take care of ourselves instead of others. We are taught by the world that this is our right and privilege, yet it destroys people and families. It broke David's life and infiltrated his family with disaster.

Jesus was just the opposite. He had the power and possibility to take and have whatever He desired, but His love for us drove Him not to take but to give. Philippians 2:3–7 explains this to us:

Do nothing from selfishness or empty conceit, but with humility of mind regard one another as more important than yourselves; do not merely look out for your own personal interests, but also for the interests of others. Have this attitude in yourselves which was also in Christ Jesus, who, although He existed in the form of God, did not regard equality with God a thing to be grasped, but emptied Himself.

Jesus operated with humility, always looking out for the interests of others. David had lived much of his life in the same humility, but power had corrupted his heart. Instead of looking out for others' interests, he looked out for his own.

Some of us have been blessed with great position and possibility, or maybe we hunger for these things. Beware. They come with a high price: our lives. If we choose to be takers instead of givers, selfish instead of generous, we may gather pleasure to ourselves for a season, but we will lose our destinies.

Jesus is looking for servant-hearted leaders who truly care for others ahead of themselves. Are you one? If so, you can count on Him to bless and multiply you and your resources so that you can touch and give life to others. If you are struggling with selfishness, bow your heart before His throne, and tell the Lord that you hunger to have His heart for others. He will begin a fresh and life-giving work in you.

——◌ PRAYER ◌——

Jesus, my flesh is selfish, and my eyes deceive me. Please touch me, Holy Spirit, so that I will see as You see and love as You love. Help me use my position and authority to bless and bring life to others, not to myself. Amen.

DAY 54

....

Loving Like Jesus

When they had finished eating, Jesus said to Simon Peter,
"Simon son of John, do you love me more than these?" "Yes, Lord,"
he said, "You know that I love you." Jesus said, "Feed my lambs."

JOHN 21:15, NIV

Peter wanted to serve Jesus in the worst possible way, yet he regularly got himself in trouble. We should all be encouraged that Jesus never gave up on him, because He will never give up on us either. When Jesus asked Peter a peculiar question about feeding His sheep, Peter must have thought one thing: *How can I ever live up to anything You set before me after I denied You at the cross?* But Jesus' love and forgiveness toward Peter enabled him to fulfill the ministry God had for him.

What Jesus was really asking Peter is, "Do you love Me?" because loving Jesus is indispensable to all ministry. If you and I are ever going to learn to love and serve others, then surrendering to Jesus and His love is not an option. It must become a lifestyle. Then loving others out of Christ's love for us will become our daily journey.

Willie Nelson and Elvis both recorded a popular song called "You Were Always on My Mind." The message of the song should be the heart of our lives as followers of Christ. What do you think was always on Jesus' mind? The Bible tells us: people were at the heart of everything Jesus did (see John 3:16). He healed them, reached out to them, loved them, and restored them. There has never been a person more preoccupied with people than Jesus was. He knew that every person would spend eternity either with Him or without Him.

Since our goal is to be like Jesus, learning to love God and love people should be our goal. Every action we take should reflect that at some level. This doesn't come easily, nor is it established overnight. When we have no desire to love another person, it can help to remind ourselves how much God loves us, despite how often we have failed Him. When our hearts are softened by Jesus' love, we can love others even if their response to us is less than kind. It's as Howard Thurman said: "When we love without being loved back, we are at least in one small way better able to understand the heart of God. Isn't that exactly what God experiences every day?"[7]

Andrew Murray offers further insight on the matter: "I must see that drawing close to God is closely bound up with my relationship to others. Failure here will cause failure there. . . . In our life with people, the one thing on which everything depends is love."[8] Today ask God to impart a deep love in your heart for Him and also for others; it will forever change you as it did Peter.

─◌ PRAYER ◌─

Holy Spirit, help me fall deeper in love with Jesus, and out of that love for You, please reveal to me anyone I need to forgive so that I might be able to love others more freely. Thank You, Father, for forgiving me of my sin. Help me forgive others who have wronged me. Amen.

DAY 55

....

Looking Ahead

Thus far the LORD has helped us.

1 SAMUEL 7:12

When Samuel built an altar between Mizpah and Shen, it pointed two ways. It pointed backward, to where Israel could see the Lord's help through sorrow, struggle, blessing, sickness, health, at home, far away, in trial, or in triumph. "The Lord has helped us!" they could proclaim. It also pointed forward, where they had yet to walk. And because the Lord had helped them in the past, they knew He would help them in days to come.

Often when we get trapped spiritually because of a past scar—some disappointment, hurt, wound, the loss of a dear friend or loved one—we find ourselves saying, "I would like to believe for so and so, but when I was sixteen, six, thirty-six, this happened to me, and I can't. It altered my possibilities." It is amazing how our yesterdays flavor our tomorrows. But here is a fact: whatever in our past has shaped our lives doesn't have any claim on our future.

Anything that may have been intimidating, restricting, negative, disappointing—it is dead! The cross declares it! The grace of the cross buries our past so that we can possess our tomorrows. "If anyone is in Christ, he is a new creation; the old has passed away; behold, the new has come" (2 Cor. 5:17, ESV).

Our destinies are in God's hand. We can delight in His promise of care. We can have confidence for the future, because He has

121

already helped us in the past, and He has promised, "He who began a good work in you will carry it on to completion until the day of Christ Jesus" (Phil. 1:6, NIV). Whenever you feel the grip of despair in your life, it is important to remember that God has promised to be with us and finish the good work He started in us.

Lay hold of God's presence, and you will realize His promises. Remember Hebrews 6:17–18: "When God wanted to guarantee his promises, he gave his word, a rock solid guarantee—God *can't* break His Word. And because His Word cannot change, the promise is likewise unchangeable" (MSG). Make that tough decision to press on into the full possibilities that Jesus has for you right now, would you?

—◦ PRAYER ◦—

Lord Jesus, forgive me for so quickly forgetting all You have done for me. Teach me, Father, to stop and look back at Your faithfulness to me over my life so that I can look forward with renewed trust and confidence in Your Spirit's work in me. Break off my past and all that hinders me from pressing into the future You have ordained for me. Amen.

DAY 56

....

Be an Encourager

There was Joseph, the one the apostles nicknamed Barnabas
(which means "Son of Encouragement"). He was from the tribe of
Levi and came from the island of Cyprus. He sold a field he owned
and brought the money to the apostles.

ACTS 4:36-37, NLT

The name "Joseph" is a fine name. In Hebrew it means "God's added blessing." This was the name for the cherished son of the patriarch Jacob. It was also the name for Jesus' earthly father. So why would the apostles give Joseph of Cypress a nickname like "Barnabas"?

Barnabas, Acts tells us, means "son of encouragement." Apparently, this Joseph was such an encourager that a new name for him was in order. When the early church needed money to underwrite its ministries, Joseph sold a field he owned and brought the money to the apostles. When Saul of Tarsus (renamed Paul) needed a friend to welcome him into the church he had once persecuted, it was Joseph who was that friend and nurtured Paul into a ministry of his own. When the church needed to send someone to encourage the new believers among the Gentiles, they sent Joseph. When young Mark needed someone to believe in him and give him a second chance to serve as a missionary, Joseph encouraged him. Is it any wonder that all Joseph's friends called him Barnabas, "son of encouragement"?

This encouraging of others is a lost art in our society. We are all taught to think about our own concerns, not those of others. Yet Jesus set the example for us when He stepped down from heaven and put us ahead of Himself so that we could live. Philippians 2:3–7 explains this clearly: "You must have the same attitude that Christ Jesus had. Though He was God, He did not think of equality with God as something to cling to. Instead, He gave up His divine privileges; He took the humble position of a slave and was born as a human being" (NLT).

God's kingdom needs leaders—those who have a heart for others and can speak up, step up, and encourage people to passionate mission and generous giving. Your faith, your story, and your passion make a difference to the ministries of the kingdom of God. Be a Barnabas! Who is within your sphere of influence—people you connect with regularly and have opportunity to encourage? Look for ways to encourage the faith of these people by sharing your witness, your passion, your faith. In doing so you multiply God's grace and influence the faithful response of others.

PRAYER

Father, it was You who changed Joseph's heart before the apostles changed his name. Do the same for me. Change my heart. Help me feel so joyful about what I am doing to make a difference in Your kingdom that I can be a witness and encouragement to others. Amen.

DAY 57

....

Remember Your Place

*They came to John and said to him, "Rabbi, He who was with you beyond
the Jordan, to whom you have testified, behold, He is baptizing and all are
coming to Him." John answered and said, "A man can receive nothing
unless it has been given him from heaven. You yourselves are my witnesses
that I said, 'I am not the Christ,' but, 'I have been sent ahead of Him.'
He who has the bride is the bridegroom; but the friend of the bridegroom,
who stands and hears him, rejoices greatly because of the bridegroom's voice.
So this joy of mine has been made full. He must increase, but I must decrease."*

JOHN 3:26-30

John the Baptist was a great man. He was the last of the prophets.
When people heard him preach, they trembled. He attracted
disciples, crowds, and the press. He even attracted the attention
of kings and queens. This is all the more amazing when we realize
that John's ministry never took place in the city but only in the
desert—far from the lights of fame and fortune, the halls of power
and prestige. This made John remarkable—a desert dweller who impacted his generation beyond anything people could have imagined.
It is important to remember this when we find ourselves thinking
that we will never be positioned to make a difference for Jesus.

When Jesus came, John knew his place—he was not the Messiah
but the Messiah's friend and forerunner. Despite being goaded by
his disciples to be jealous of Jesus' early success in ministry, John
remained steadfast in his sense of place within God's plan. He rejoiced in the following Jesus attracted. He even helped some of his

own disciples join with Jesus. John 3:22–30 is John's explanation of his own role to his disciples: "Now my joy is complete. Jesus must increase, and I must decrease."

Have you discovered this truth yet? Most of us think joy increases as *we* increase—as our wealth, prestige, influence, and power grow. But the opposite is true. Lasting joy is not found at the top of the corporate mountain or the pinnacle of power. Joy is not a reward of accomplishment. True joy is found where John the Baptist found it: in right relationship to Jesus Christ.

Are you ready to find complete joy? Jesus must continue to increase in significance and lordship in our lives, while we and our plans and ambitions must decrease.

—◦ PRAYER ◦—

Holy Spirit, increase and decrease are both in Your hand. Please lead me to find joy and abundant living as I give my life more fully to You. Teach me the lessons of surrender that I must learn so that You can be all You desire to be to me. Amen.

Rightly Relating to People

Just as we have been approved by God to be entrusted with the gospel,
so we speak, not as pleasing men, but God who examines our hearts.

1 THESSALONIANS 2:4

How we respond to someone else being blessed speaks about the condition of our hearts. It's the heart that matters. How do you know where your heart is focused? When a coworker gets the promotion you longed for, how do you respond? When a friend gets into the college you applied for, how do you feel about it? When someone else gets pregnant and you have been trying for years, what goes through your heart?

We need to ask ourselves some questions: Am I looking to God or to people to meet my needs? Am I angry and resentful of people who don't meet my needs? Do I blame others for my circumstances? People will almost always disappoint us in one way or another. If we are committed to Jesus and asking Him daily to meet all our needs, should we ever resent another person getting blessed? When we feel anger or resentment toward others' successes, we are likely not living in faith but in the flesh. We are attempting to make our own way instead of believing that God is a way maker for us.

When we don't stay on our number—when we want to live somebody else's life—we are not submitted to Christ. His Spirit is not leading us. We have allowed our focus to move away from Jesus and onto others.

A spirit of pride or poverty may be working in our lives if we do not stay focused on God. A spirit of pride tells us, "I deserved that promotion more than that person." A spirit of poverty tells us, "I am angry, because God will never do that for me." We have little faith and no perspective as to how God loves all His kids and blesses all of us in due time. The spirit of pride says, "I deserve more," and poverty says, "I will never get any." But a heart focused on the Lord says, "Thank You, Jesus, for blessing my friend!"

When you find your heart straying away from the Lord and your focus moving toward others, stop and bow your heart. Tell God you are grateful that you are you. Tell Him you are thankful that He has His eye on you and on your circumstances and your destiny.

⁓ PRAYER ⁓

Father, thank You that You are a God of blessings! Each time I see You bless someone else, remind me to give thanks for Your giving heart. Holy Spirit, teach me to be still and know that my Father has His eye on me and that He will meet me where I need to be met. Amen.

DAY 59

....

No Regrets and Tons of Mercy

Now, my son, the LORD be with you that you may be successful, and build
the house of the LORD your God just as He has spoken concerning you.
Only the LORD give you discretion and understanding, and give you
charge over Israel, so that you may keep the law of the LORD your God.
Then you will prosper, if you are careful to observe the statutes and the
ordinances which the LORD commanded Moses concerning Israel.
Be strong and courageous, do not fear nor be dismayed.

1 CHRONICLES 22:11-13

Instead of sitting on the sidelines of life and pouting over the loss
of his dream to build the temple, David made it a point to bless
what God was doing in his son Solomon. As king, he could have
made the transition of kingship to his son difficult, as many men
with smaller hearts have done. David, however, not only made his
circumstances a blessing, but he went beyond the call to make sure
that everyone around him would succeed.

That is a true sign of greatness: no insecurity, no fear of others' success. Move with God! Move with power. Jump into what
the Holy Spirit is doing, even if He is doing it with someone other
than you. Don't be afraid of losing out—we can't lose out when we
jump in and bless others. Solomon was going to build the temple,
not David, so the only question was, would David help build and
bless, or would he let the facts be a painful reminder of his own
selfishness and failure?

We all face these types of situations at work, at school, on the team, in our neighborhoods. This is life. Let Jesus' light shine through you by giving yourself and your desires up for the King and the kingdom.

Look at David's own words, because they are words of greatness. Read them slowly and closely, and ask the Holy Spirit to give you a heart like this:

"With great pains I have prepared for the house of the LORD 100,000 talents of gold and 1,000,000 talents of silver, and bronze and iron beyond weight, for they are in great quantity; also timber and stone I have prepared, and you may add to them. . . . Arise and work, and may the LORD be with you."

David also commanded all the leaders of Israel to help his son Solomon, saying, "Is not the LORD your God with you? And has He not given you rest on every side? For He has given the inhabitants of the land into my hand, and the land is subdued before the LORD and before His people. Now set your heart and your soul to seek the LORD your God; arise, therefore, and build the sanctuary of the LORD God, so that you may bring the ark of the covenant of the LORD and the holy vessels of God into the house that is to be built for the name of the LORD." (1 Chron. 22:14–19)

—◌ PRAYER ◌—

David's heart is amazing. Father, please impart a heart like that to me, a heart after God, a heart that makes other people better, a heart that shines Your light in the darkness of my world. Teach me never to fear blessing others and making them a success. Thank You, Lord. Amen.

DAY 60

....

All In with Jesus

The kingdom of heaven is like treasure hidden in a field.
When a man found it, he hid it again, and then in his joy went
and sold all he had and bought that field. Again, the kingdom of
heaven is like a merchant looking for fine pearls. When he found
one of great value, he went away and sold everything he had
and bought it.

M ATTHEW 13:44–46, NIV

Taking a stand against those who oppose us is something most of us would rather not do in this day and age of correctness. Over the course of his life, Joshua had watched the people of Israel fill their lives with activities and enticements that crowded out the life of God, but in his last days he asked the people to consider who they would live for: "If serving the LORD seems undesirable to you, then choose for yourselves this day whom you will serve. . . . As for me and my household, we will serve the LORD" (Josh. 24:15, NIV).

God is looking for people who will be all in and nothing less. Taking a stand and making a decision to live for Jesus is not popular today, but really, it's never been popular to live for God, because it makes people uncomfortable. We must choose for ourselves life or death, healing or hurt, hope or the crooked road that many of us have been traveling.

When we are faced with tough choices, we should weigh them out, the risk versus the reward. The reward Christ offers us is not comparable to anything in this world. That is why the parables in

Matthew 13 about selling all we have to get the treasure changed my life: "The kingdom of heaven is like treasure hidden in a field. When a man found it, he hid it again, and then in his joy went and sold all he had and bought that field." Overwhelmed by his discovery, the man who found the treasure went and sold all he had to buy the field where the treasure lay. He made a wise decision, and that is what Jesus was telling the story to communicate: if we give up all we have in this world to secure the treasure of God's kingdom, we make a wise decision, because God's kingdom is the only thing in this world worth the investment of our entire lives!

This is a difficult lesson for humans to learn, isn't it? It is tough for us to resist the allure of temporal self-centered desires and ambitions and take a stand against the popular opinions of our day. Take time today and ask yourself, "Am I all in with Jesus?"

PRAYER

Lord, thank You for calling me to live above this world's standards. Holy Spirit, give me courage to stand for You, like Joshua did, when people around me are living for lesser things. Father, help me see that Your kingdom is worth the investment of everything I own. Thank You, Lord. Amen.

Fulfilling Your Destiny

God is calling us to live extraordinary lives.
The time to do that is not next year or next month
or even tomorrow—it is now!
Don't limit yourself. Make a difference!
Seize the day for the King and the kingdom.

DAY 61

God Has Given You Amazing Possibility

What is man that You take thought of him, and the son of man that You care for him? Yet You have made him a little lower than God, and You crown him with glory and majesty! You make him to rule over the works of Your hands; You have put all things under his feet.

PSALM 8:4-6

God has an incredible view of you and me—a view from above. Psalm 8 says that He has crowned us with glory and majesty. Wow, what a crazy statement. God has set us apart from all creation and put His image in us. He has given us authority and possibility to touch and change destiny in this life and in the next.

Are you using your God-given glory for His good? Have you chosen to make a difference in eternity? Do you value people more than things? Do you sacrifice to touch others? Do you live daily as if you believe that you are the crown of all creation? Our decisions about these things impact how we live and what we value.

We all have routines and habits, but not all our habits give life. The old proverb says, "Sow a thought, reap an action; sow an action, reap a habit; sow a habit, reap a character; sow a character, reap a destiny." Are your habits building you into the person you were created to become? Ask yourself what a spiritually mature servant of God looks like—is that what *you* look like? Bad habits are tough to break, but spiritual growth requires persistence, passion, and patience.

Proverbs says, "Whoever practices discipline is on the way to life" (Prov. 10:17, GWT). Jesus was God, yet He formed habits while on the earth. We are told in Luke 5:16 that "Jesus often withdrew to lonely places and prayed" (NIV). Sometimes it feels impossible for us to change, but God can change us. If we belong to Jesus, He has set destiny before us. He desires to draw us into deep relationship with Him and then use us to touch others. Jesus prayed for us,

> The glory which You have given Me I have given to them, that they may be one, just as We are one; I in them and You in Me, that they may be perfected in unity, so that the world may know that You sent Me, and loved them, even as You have loved Me. (John 17:22-23)

God has put His glory on us for a reason larger than us. Today ask the Lord to give you the grace and desire to sit with Him and allow Him to touch you. Turn to Him and surrender daily to Him; let Him bind your heart to His so that you can fulfill your destiny.

PRAYER

Jesus, I am stunned to think of Your glory in my life. Thank You for desiring deep relationship with me. Draw me to You, and teach me to live in Your heart with Your values, not mine. Teach me to come to You daily and set my heart before You so that I can fulfill all You have for me. Amen.

Building Heart and Skill

*Saul's servants then said to him, . . . "Let [your servants] seek
a man who is a skillful player on the harp; and it shall come
about when the evil spirit from God is on you, that he shall
play the harp with his hand, and you will be well." So Saul
said to his servants, "Provide for me now a man who can play
well and bring him to me." Then one of the young men said,
"Behold, I have seen a son of Jesse the Bethlehemite who is a
skillful musician, . . . and the LORD is with him."*

1 SAMUEL 16:15-18

God is building two things in us as we grow in our service to Him: heart and skill. Both of these take time to develop. Most of us understand that the Lord is developing our hearts, but many of us miss the fact that God is also working to impart skill to us.

God has gifted us with spiritual gifts. We may not know what our gifts are or understand where they came from, but if we know Jesus, the Holy Spirit has and is imparting gifts into our lives: "About the gifts of the Spirit, brothers and sisters, I do not want you to be uninformed. . . . There are different kinds of gifts, but the same Spirit distributes them. There are different kinds of service, but the same Lord. There are different kinds of working, but in all of them and in everyone it is the same God at work. Now to each one the manifestation of the Spirit is given for the common good" (1 Cor. 12:1, 4–7, NIV).

God gives us spiritual gifts so we can touch other people. They flow out of us in a supernatural way, because they are spiritual. David had spiritual gifts imparted to him by the Lord, and then God shaped those gifts in David until he had skill. It was at that point that David's gifts began to impact his destiny.

When we come to the Lord, we should ask Him to impart to us all the gifts He has for us. Then we must allow Him to shape and mold those gifts. This takes time. But in the everyday school of life, the Holy Spirit will hone our gifting and impart skill to us. David's gifting, shaped by his skill, opened the doors to his destiny. David was gifted as a musician, and his times alone in worship with the Lord built skill into this gifting. It was that skill that first opened the door to the throne room of the king for him.

Ask the Holy Spirit to impart His gifts to you, and then come to Him daily and ask for His timing in shaping those gifts and releasing you to touch others with them. Be patient as you wait for the Lord to shape your gifts. Proverbs 18:16 promises us, "A man's gift makes room for him and brings him before great men."

—⌘ PRAYER ⌘—

Father, please impart to me all the gifts You have for me. Teach me to use them to glorify You as I touch others. Bring skill to me, Lord—not the skill of the world but skill that would please Your heart. Amen.

....

Be Who God Made You to Be

*Saul gave David his own armor—a bronze helmet and a coat of
mail. David put it on, strapped the sword over it, and took a step or
two to see what it was like, for he had never worn such things before.
"I can't go in these," he protested to Saul. "I'm not used to them."
So David took them off again. He picked up five smooth stones from
a stream and put them into his shepherd's bag. Then, armed only
with his shepherd's staff and sling, he started across the valley
to fight the Philistine.*

1 SAMUEL 17:38-40, NLT

How often have we felt that we just had to conform to what
someone else wanted us to be? There are certainly times to be
a team player, but there are also times when others press us or we
press ourselves into a mold that is not from God. That is part of
the story of David and Goliath. First Saul tried to persuade David
not to fight the giant—he discouraged him. Then when it was clear
that David was all in and there was no way to prevent him from
entering the battle, Saul told him to fight it Saul's way.

It is important to note that the Spirit of the Lord was not leading Saul at this time. The Spirit had departed from him (see 1 Sam.
16:14), so Saul was operating in his flesh. It is crucial for us to dis-
cern the counsel given to us. Is it from God or man? Saul's counsel

that David put on the king's armor was from man, not God. It is true that God's counsel—that David face the giant with the sling-shot and stones he was accustomed to—seemed on the surface to make no sense at all, but it was right for David.

David's confidence was not self-confidence—that would have been foolish. It was a confidence born in his times alone with his heavenly Father. David took off Saul's armor and put on God's: he picked up five stones and took his sling and staff and went out to the valley to battle the giant. He wasn't dressed like any other soldier on the battlefield that day. He was dressed the way God wanted him to be dressed, and he was dressed for victory!

Each day as you come to the Lord, ask Him to confirm His hand in you. Then be intentional to spend time with other believers who are ahead of you in the journey of faith, and let them speak into your life and confirm what God is saying to you.

PRAYER

Jesus, so often I allow others to shape my life in their image instead of allowing You to transform me into Your image. Please forgive me, Lord. I see clearly that there will be times when You ask me to step out and take a risk—when You ask me not to conform to others' expectations so that You can transform the situation. Holy Spirit, impart a spirit of discernment to me so that I will know when You are speaking to me. Amen.

DAY 64

Giving into God's Kingdom

The disciples came to Him and said, "This place is desolate and the hour is already late; so send the crowds away, that they may go into the villages and buy food for themselves." But Jesus said to them, "They do not need to go away; you give them something to eat!"

MATTHEW 14:15-16

Jesus had been with the crowds all day, ministering to people's needs. Frankly, the disciples were tired of dealing with all the people. "Send the crowds away," they told Jesus. "Let them go home and take care of themselves. Surely You don't expect us to be responsible for their needs."

When we as God's people are challenged with the needs of people around us, it is easy for us to say to each other, "Let's just send the crowds away. Surely it's not our responsibility to minister to all these needs." But don't try saying that to Jesus. Jesus' response was, and still is, clear: "*They* do not need to go away. *You* give them something to eat."

"A crowd of more than five thousand—how can we meet that kind of need? It's overwhelming!" the disciples were saying. But one boy in the crowd saw the need and, determined to do what he could, gave five loaves and two fish. It must have taken all the disciples' composure to receive this boy's gift with gratefulness and seriousness and not laugh in his face. What was this small gift among so many people? But Jesus took the gift and blessed it, and the crowd of more than five thousand was fed.

David Livingston, the great missionary to Africa (one of my favorite heroes, who is buried under the floor at Westminster Abbey), wrote, "I will place no value on anything I have or may possess except in relation to the kingdom of Christ. If anything will advance the interests of the kingdom, it shall be given away or kept, only as by giving or keeping it I shall most promote the glory of Him to whom I owe all my hopes in time or eternity." God desires for us to grasp the value of His kingdom and experience the adventure of giving of ourselves to build that kingdom. In fact, the Bible contains more than 2,300 verses that deal with managing, multiplying, and giving of our lives and resources into the kingdom of God.

Every dimension of God's character reveals His giving nature: our Father freely gave His Son; Jesus freely gave His life; then He freely gave of His Spirit to empower and lead us into truth. Why should we give toward others' needs? Because God does, and He offers us the opportunity to partner with Him in His work in the world today. No one can make up for your part—you have something to give to God's work that only you can provide. Ask the Holy Spirit what He wants you to do as you steward your time, talent, and resources so that you can further His kingdom through your own adventure in generosity.

—⌒ PRAYER ⌒—

Lord, make me a willing partner in Your kingdom. Teach me to believe bigger than my circumstances and situations. Multiply my gifts so that they will make more difference than I ever imagined they could. Thank You, Lord. Amen.

DAY 65

....

Partnering with God

LORD our God, all this abundance that we have provided
for building you a temple for your Holy Name comes from
your hand, and all of it belongs to you.

1 CHRONICLES 29:16, NIV

God wants to partner with people to do His work. He can do it without us, but instead He chooses to do it through us. He moves in us with possibility and gifting and skill and then asks us to surrender those gifts back to Him. It was the same in David's day.

Having invited the people of Israel to give toward the temple that his son Solomon would build for the Lord, David received what is likely the largest building offering ever taken. Historians estimate the monetary value at somewhere over 300 million dollars. King David rejoiced greatly at this offering (who wouldn't have?!), but he did not thank the people for it. He was careful not to lose sight of a truth revealed to us in James 1:17: "Every perfect gift is from above."

All that we have to offer our Father is actually His already. He shares His wealth with us so that we might become more like Him as we learn to give back into the work of His kingdom. I once heard Pastor Jack Hayford put it this way in a message he preached: "When we worship with our tithing, we are giving spiritual acknowledgment to this: life is a gift of God, and everything we have comes from God."

We are to manage the gifts God has given us so that His generosity can flow through us. We are not called to be reservoirs but rivers, because God wants to flow through us. We often look at trust in terms of whether or not God can be trusted, but maybe we need to consider whether God can trust us. Can He trust us to manage our gifts to invest in others' lives when their eternity is at stake?

Jesus told a story of a man who gave talents to each of his workers and then left on a trip. At the end of the story, the man blessed those workers who had been faithful with his money and rewarded them for their diligent work (see Matt. 25:14–30). No doubt Jesus told this story to help us understand that He has likewise trusted us with gifts, skills, and resources and asks us to steward them wisely to serve others.

We are just stewards. We get to watch over all God has given us for a season of our lives. But it is never ours; it is always His. Today stop and ask yourself, "Am I investing God's gifts to me wisely to touch and change others' lives?"

―◦ PRAYER ◦―

Oh Jesus, I am so grateful for Your abundant gifts to me. Help me remember that everything I give You is Yours already. Forgive me for not easily releasing my grip on all You have given me. Please teach me how to give back to You some of what You have given me. Amen.

DAY 66

God First

When the LORD brings you to the land . . . and gives it to you,
you shall devote to the LORD the first offspring of every womb,
and the first offspring of every beast that you own.

EXODUS 13:11–12

We have taught the principle of putting God first at Water of Life Community Church for a long time because it is so crucial to making any headway with Jesus. If we want to grow, we have to figure this out. Exodus 23:19 reads, "You shall bring the choice first fruits of your soil into the house of the LORD your God." Also, in the account of the fall of Jericho, the Lord instructed the Israelites not to keep any of the spoils found there because it was the first city they conquered.

Many of us somehow think that this principle of giving to God first is negotiable. I hear this all the time: "God understands when I don't do His things first." Well, He may understand that we are busy, and certainly He is graceful and merciful, but none of us gets a pass here. Either we figure out that God is God and doesn't want to be sixth or sixteenth on our lists, or we miss out on a huge amount of blessing that comes from being positioned to be touched and used by Him.

In Matthew 6:33 Jesus kindly but clearly said the same thing when He declared, "Seek first His kingdom and His righteousness, and all these things will be added to you." This principle is true whether it regards our time, talent, or resources. The old adage "first things first" holds biblical truth.

The Word speaks of money and possessions more than two thousand times, because God can use money as a test of our faith. Placing our money in the Lord's hands requires us to exercise faith that He will meet any shortfall we might incur; this is different from waiting to see if we have enough for ourselves and then giving Him our leftovers.

The Word teaches that the firstborn is to be either sacrificed or redeemed by the sacrifice of a lamb (see Exod. 34:20). In Scripture at least thirteen times the Lord declares that the firstborn are His.[1] He demonstrated this in Egypt in the final plague when He struck down the unredeemed firstborn of every Egyptian, even as He gave His people instructions to apply the blood of a lamb to their doorposts so that death would pass over their firstborn sons.

When we sacrifice in order to give to the Lord, He will redeem our sacrifice. Jesus illustrated this principle when He said, "Whoever wishes to save his life will lose it; but whoever loses his life for My sake will find it" (Matt. 16:25). Giving to the Lord sacrificially demonstrates that we have put Him first.

⤳ PRAYER ⤲

Father, You are so graceful and kind. Please forgive me for not putting You first in everything. Teach me to put You first in my daily living so that I will become the vessel of life You created me to be. Holy Spirit, please give me a heart that puts the Father first in everything. Amen.

DAY 67

Stewards in God's House

A man can receive nothing
unless it has been given him from heaven.

JOHN 3:27

The concept of stewardship comes from the Father. He gives us good gifts and asks us to participate with Him in a destiny that impacts others. You see, the word "steward" actually means "he who is over the house." It refers to a special servant whom a wealthy owner in Bible times would put over the affairs of his home. Joseph was one of those guys, a steward put in charge of Potiphar's home (see Gen. 39:1-6). His job was to make sure everything was in order—food on the table, oil in the lamps, everything in the house running rightly.

God calls us stewards too. He has put us in charge of His house! He doesn't expect us to accumulate stuff for ourselves; He expects us to build His house, His kingdom, with the resources we have been given. The heart of stewardship is recognizing that we're not the owners of the resources we've received. We are entrusted by the owner to make sure His house is running rightly and to use our resources according to His wishes and His will. Paul makes this clear: "It is required of stewards that one be found trustworthy" (1 Cor. 4:2).

There was a time when everyone in the world believed that the planets in our solar system revolved around the earth. Today we know that the earth is not the center of the solar system, but we wouldn't know it by the way people live. Many act as if they are the center of the solar system. We are all taught that we are consumers who deserve to get whatever we want. Unfortunately, this attitude has impacted the church today. Many have come to see the church as a commodity to be consumed rather than a place to give of ourselves. This attitude hinders all that God wants to do with His people to make us others focused.

Our greatest challenge is to live our lives as Jesus did: for others. He served others, loved others, healed others, and He challenges everyone who knows Him to do the same. When God asks us to give into His kingdom so that He can touch others through our service, He is asking us to live not as consumers but as disciples, people who have been taught the heart of Jesus for others.

What is the difference between an owner and a steward? This is a crucial question. The owner makes the decisions, and the steward carries them out according to the owner's will. Our entire journey with Jesus depends on this principle. He cannot be our King if we do not understand how we are to steward His stuff. Our mission field is others, and God has given us gifts and resources to serve others. Let's touch our world for our King!

—◦ PRAYER ◦—

Father, teach me my role as Your steward, and help me cultivate a greater sense of stewardship in my own life. Holy Spirit, this is certainly a work You can do and desire to do in me. Help me surrender to it and allow You to have Your way in me. Amen.

DAY 68

....

When Leaders Lead

The people rejoiced at the willing response of their leaders,
for they had given freely and wholeheartedly to the LORD.
David the king also rejoiced greatly.

1 CHRONICLES 29:9

When Water of Life first talked about raising funds for our building project for a new sanctuary and to pay off the balance of our mortgage, I did something rather risky. I told the church that my wife, Gale, and I had sat down and talked about our commitment to this whole endeavor and our need to lead and decided that we would give our savings to the campaign.

We had plans for that money, but we have learned that the journey with Jesus is an adventure. When we decide to obey in faith, we get to sit by and watch Him provide for our needs or wants in some miraculous way we could never have dreamed of. We believed that Jesus was in our building project 100 percent, and we could never have asked the people of Water of Life to sacrifice if we weren't willing to do so as well.

Wholehearted surrender is often difficult. But when we do surrender ourselves to God, we are often surprised by the life we find. We discover a flood of joy, a lifting of burdens from our hearts, a hopefulness that comes only when we "let go and let God." Willingness is the key. When we offer willingly with wholeheartedness, as the leaders of Israel did, the Holy Spirit is released in us to bring life. This is the law of the kingdom: give, and God will give back; hold out, and we will miss out!

Giving is a lifestyle, a matter of the heart, and it encompasses far more than money. It is about our hearts and attitudes toward God and others more than the amount we give. John D. Rockefeller once said, "I never would have been able to tithe the first million dollars I ever made if I had not tithed my first salary, which was $1.50 a week." God trusted Rockefeller with millions of dollars but not before He had trusted him with $1.50 a week. Jesus said in Luke 6:10 that those who are faithful in a little thing can be trusted with much.

David and his leaders blessed the people by leading the way, and that is what leaders are to do today. The Bible challenges all believers to give faithfully, regularly, deliberately, sacrificially, cheerfully, extravagantly, and even hilariously. Ask yourself today, "Am I growing to give faithfully and cheerfully to touch others?" Let us rejoice as we, by faith, willingly release ourselves to Jesus and His destiny for us.

—<୭ PRAYER ଦ—

Lord, help me become a giving person. It is so easy to expect others to give and not ever give myself. Empower me by Your Holy Spirit to give to my friends, my family, and You, my Father. Lord, give me a willing heart that is surrendered to You! Amen.

DAY 69

....

Anointed for Service

You have anointed my head with oil; my cup overflows.
Surely goodness and lovingkindness will follow me all the days of
my life, and I will dwell in the house of the LORD forever.

PSALM 23:5-6

David's life pivoted one day. It began with the same old hum-
drum of shepherding. But when our hearts are surrendered
before the Lord, our days will not all be the same old, same old.
First Samuel 16:12-13 describes what took place:

> Samuel said to Jesse, "Send and bring him; for we will not
> sit down until he comes here." So he sent and brought him
> in. Now he was ruddy, with beautiful eyes and a handsome
> appearance. And the LORD said, "Arise, anoint him; for
> this is he." Then Samuel took the horn of oil and anoint-
> ed him in the midst of his brothers; and the Spirit of the
> LORD came mightily upon David from that day forward.

No doubt when David wrote, "You have anointed my head with
oil," he was thinking of this moment—a moment that set his destiny. Why should this matter to us? Because the Holy Spirit desires
to anoint each of us who call on Jesus' name. The word "anoint" in
Greek, the language of the New Testament, is *chrio*. It is where we
get *Christos*, meaning "Messiah," or "Anointed One." It is the title
given to Jesus: Jesus Christ, or Jesus *Christos*. So when David said

he was anointed, he literally said, "I have received the deep touch of the Messiah."

The word "anoint" also means "to rub in," so it is really the deep touch of Jesus rubbed into our lives, the outpouring of His presence on us. Jesus spoke of the need for this in Luke 4:17–21:

> He opened the book and found the place where it was written, "The Spirit of the Lord is upon Me, because He anointed Me to preach the gospel to the poor. He has sent Me to proclaim release to the captives, and recovery of sight to the blind, to set free those who are oppressed, to proclaim the favorable year of the Lord." And He closed the book, gave it back to the attendant and sat down; and the eyes of all in the synagogue were fixed on Him. And He began to say to them, "Today this Scripture has been fulfilled in your hearing."

Before Jesus ever moved with power in ministry, the Holy Spirit anointed Him. How much more do we need this anointing if we are going to touch a dead and dying world? Many of us have been taught to fear the touch of God's Spirit, but we need not fear the Holy Spirit. He is the Spirit of Jesus.

Do you want more of Jesus today? Bow down, and invite Him to anoint you with His oil. Ask Him to pour out His Spirit on you, and then watch Him use you to touch and heal, restore and renew life in others.

⎯⎯ PRAYER ⎯⎯

Father, today I bow before You and ask that You pour out Your Spirit on me. I believe that You have a deep desire to touch my life and use me to touch others. I understand that without Your Spirit's power I can do nothing to further Your name, so please anoint me. Amen.

DAY 70

....

Do You Hear God's Call?

Speak, LORD, for Your servant is listening.

1 SAMUEL 3:9

In the time of Samuel, the Bible says, "Word from the LORD was rare in those days, visions were infrequent" (1 Sam. 3:1). It is easy for us to feel the same way today. Which of us has heard God call our name? Which of us has heard God speak a word to us? And what great godly visions drive our lives?

Most people seem to think that the word of the Lord is rare, that it comes only to people like pastors, who are somehow specially called. Most people seem to think that God has no word, no calling, no vision for them. But maybe, like the boy Samuel, we simply are not listening well. We hear someone calling our name and tugging at our heart, and we assume that the someone is just a leader in our lives making a fuss again. Perhaps we need to listen better for a word from God. Perhaps it is not a word from God that is rare but rather faithful listening from those who would serve God.

Every Christian has a calling. In fact, every Christian has several callings as well as God-given gifts, graces, and blessings to respond to those callings. And God is still speaking to His people about those callings!

Every Christian is called to be a faithful steward of the talents and time and resources God has blessed us with. Being a faithful steward is a personal calling—a word from the Lord. It is a calling that comes with each of our names attached to it. It is a calling that only each individual believer can make a decision about. We can ignore that calling completely. We can brush it off by responding to it only in minimal ways. Or, recognizing God's claim over our lives, we can wake up and listen for God's voice to our own hearts.

The Lord has a word for you. He has a vision for His kingdom. Are you listening for His word? Consider all the places where you can hear God's word (in Scripture, worship, prayer, other faithful people, etc.), then go to Him and say, "Speak to me, Lord. I am Your servant. I am listening to hear from You."

PRAYER

Jesus, there are a lot of noises out there today, a lot of voices that demand to be heard. Please teach me not only to say Samuel's prayer, "Speak, for Your servant is listening," but actually to listen for Your word, Lord, and obey what You say. Thank You, Father. Amen.

DAY 71

Giving Yourself First to God

*They gave themselves first of all to the Lord,
and then by the will of God also to us.*

2 CORINTHIANS 8:5, NIV

Have you ever watched a T-ball game where the children are just beginning to learn baseball? Sometimes a child is so excited to hit the ball off the tee that he or she runs directly to third base and then races back to home plate to score. Too often we shortcut the ground rules of giving to God's work, like the child who runs directly to third. We rush off by offering money or service to our church or to some ministry; but to make a true investment of our hearts into the kingdom of God and the lives of others, we have to go all the way around and touch all the bases.

This means that we must establish our faith before we consider the practical aspects of serving. In 2 Corinthians 8:5, Paul says of the Macedonian church, "They gave themselves *first* of all to the Lord, and *then* by the will of God also to us" (NIV). Getting to first means determining our level of commitment to God before deciding what it is He wants us to give or do in His kingdom.

First things first. They gave themselves *first* to the Lord. That is the place to begin a conversation about serving the Lord. Remember, God is all about relationship. He knows that our hearts follow our treasure, and that is why He longs to be first in our journeys. Then our hearts will be inclined to follow Him. Instead of rushing to our budgets or our schedules or our abilities when we think of investing in God's work, we should answer these questions: What has God called me to be? What has God called me to do? What is God doing in my church? How is God working in my life? How can I give myself more fully to God?

Stewardship doesn't have as much to do with our possessions or our time or our skills as it does with partnering with God from our hearts. God is after us. This is nothing new; He is crazy about us and wants us to respond to His love for us. This is stewardship—giving ourselves to Him.

—✏ PRAYER ✐—

Jesus, let me first give myself more fully to You. Then let my decisions grow out of what I believe and what Your Spirit is doing in me—out of what You are calling me to be and do. Then remind me that You want me to give myself to others who are lost and hurting. Amen.

DAY 72

....

Growing in God's Heart

Your kingdom come. Your will be done, on earth as it is in heaven.

MATTHEW 6:10

I often like to say that God is a giver, because He is. He just gives and gives and gives to us—mercy and grace and healing and life! Unfortunately, learning to give is tough for many of us. Giving time, money, and resources can become a real battle.

Many years ago I learned a priceless lesson from my brother-in-law. I mentioned to him that I had a date coming up with a girl I really liked, and immediately he responded, "Borrow my car. That will make your night an awesome evening." Well, his car was a brand-new 240Z Datsun sports car. I was in shock because I was twenty years old, and I couldn't believe he would even consider loaning that car to me. I decided to ask him why he would do such a wild and generous thing. His answer changed my life forever. He simply said, "The Lord has been really clear with me: don't own anything you can't share or give away." Oh my, what a thought: don't own anything I wouldn't share or give away! I borrowed the car, but I got a life lesson that week. God began to teach me about generosity, about living and loving the way He does.

Paul wrote about giving, "They gave themselves first of all to the Lord, and then *by the will of God* also to us" (2 Cor. 8:5, NIV).

Seeking God's will means asking God to get involved in our decisions and in our lives! Seeking God's will means inviting God's input and guidance regarding our service to Him and others. It means genuinely asking, "What would You do through me, Lord, to make Your will happen?" Then it means yielding and surrendering to His still, small voice inside us. Until we learn how to listen and obey, we will never grow deep into our Father's heart. And remember, our Father's heart is a giving heart, so we should never be surprised when He asks us to give our time, our counsel, or our finances to help others.

How do we ask for God's guidance and seek His will? How do we invite God to participate in our lives? These things happen as we intentionally spend time in prayer, listening to the Spirit and reading the Word. Giving ourselves or our time or our money means discovering and acting within a sense of God's passions and His heart.

PRAYER

Lord, I want to honor Your name. Speak to me! Let Your will be done in me and through me. Let Your kingdom come here in my life. Create a hunger in me that only You can fulfill! Thank You, Holy Spirit, for working in my life. Amen.

DAY 73

....

Living the Father's Heart

Since you excel in everything—in faith, in speech, in knowledge,
in complete earnestness and in the love we have kindled in you—
see that you also excel in this grace of giving. I am not
commanding you, but I want to test the sincerity of your love.

2 CORINTHIANS 8:7-8

Paul is so passionate about God's heart and God's desire for us to help others and really love them. See, when God asks us to give, it is often a test, as Paul says here: "I am testing the genuineness of your love." Our love for others has to grow and pass the test if we are going to grow into our Father's heart. Sometimes our hearts say no, but we sense God saying yes. In times like these I have learned to obey and then watch my feelings change. When we invest in others or in the kingdom of God, our feelings will catch up. They may not agree at first, but they will turn toward the Father's heart.

This is where praxis comes in. "Praxis" is an interesting word, one of those big words I learned in seminary! Praxis is the point at which our faith and our actions intersect. Praxis is the point at which what we believe and what we do join together. To put it simply, praxis means walking the walk as well as talking the talk!

Talking to the church in Corinth, Paul knew that there was no formula for giving. In fact, he realized that he could not command

Into the Heart of God

anyone about exactly how each person was supposed to give. Giving has to grow from the heart. There is no one correct plan for everyone. If there was a formula for us to make sacrificial decisions by, giving wouldn't be a test. Making faith real is a unique journey for every individual. Our praxis is our way of walking the walk. But as Paul well knew, giving is a test of the heart in action, a test of the genuineness of love. Giving is where what we believe gets real.

There comes a time when we need to get practical about God's blessings in our lives and what we can and will do to support God's work with our finances, our time, and our relationships. When we do, we grow—surprisingly, we grow into our Father's heart!

⤙ PRAYER ⤚

Father, praxis is when what I believe meets what I do, and honestly, this is when walking with You gets tough for me sometimes. Holy Spirit, empower me today to live what I believe at work, at school, at home. Make me to be a doer of Your Word. Amen.

DAY 74

....

Discerning God's Voice

Saul chose 3,000 elite troops from all Israel and went to search for
David and his men near the rocks of the wild goats. At the place where
the road passes some sheepfolds, Saul went into a cave to relieve himself.
But as it happened, David and his men were hiding farther back in that
very cave! "Now's your opportunity!" David's men whispered to him.
"Today the LORD is telling you, 'I will certainly put your enemy into
your power, to do with as you wish.'" So David crept forward
and cut off a piece of the hem of Saul's robe.

1 SAMUEL 24:2-4, NLT

Many Christians live on the surface of their relationship with Jesus. For them being led by the Spirit means that God will open or close doors to show them His will. Beloved, this can be true, but far too often it is not the way of the Lord, as this story about David shows us. See, open doors can happen in many ways and for many reasons. Just because a door is open does not necessarily mean we are to walk through it. The door may have opened due to our skill, not God's will. It may have opened to test us, not to move us.

When Saul wandered into this cave to use the bathroom, it would seem at first quite obvious that the Lord had put him into David's hands so that David could kill him. Saul was a direct threat to David and to David's destiny as king. David's men read it this way: "Now's your opportunity! Today the Lord is giving your enemy into your hands!" But they were all wrong, and had David listened to them, he would have thwarted his destiny.

How many times have you wanted God to say yes to something you desired, and when you sought counsel from your friends, they all concurred that your desire was from the Lord? Certainly they meant well, but beware, because opportunity does not mean permission, and license doesn't mean liberty to move. The door may very well be open, but that does not mean that the Lord wants you to walk through it. What made David great was his ability to listen to the Spirit rather than the people. This is the same thing Jesus wants to do in us: lead us by His voice through His Spirit's work in us.

Jesus will test our hearts to build us into His image. He did that this day with Saul when He had him wander into the very cave where David and his men were hiding. He was testing David so that He could later use him deeply. He will test us as well, in giving, in generosity, in honoring others. Walk humbly and worshipfully before the Lord, and He will direct your steps into paths of righteousness for His name's sake.

——⟶ PRAYER ⟵——

Jesus, when I am running ahead of You, slow me down, please. Remind me that You and You alone mark my steps and set my path. Lord, I hunger to walk in Your ways, not mine, so please teach me, Holy Spirit, to slow down and listen to Your still, small voice as You direct me. Amen.

DAY 75

Wrestling in Prayer

*Epaphras . . . is always wrestling in prayer for you, that you may
stand firm in all the will of God, mature and fully assured.*

COLOSSIANS 4:12, NIV

Wrestling is an ancient sport. In the first century wrestlers
struggled for their lives, not for TV ratings. In the language
of their day, the wrestling ring was called the *agone*, and the wrestlers were called antagonists.

This is the word image Paul used to describe the work of prayer
by a spiritual leader of the Colossian church, Epaphras. Paul told
the church that Epaphras was wrestling in prayer for them. In other
words, Epaphras agonized in prayer for them. What a powerful
image. It is also a biblical image, seen in the picture of Jacob wrestling with the angel all night for a blessing (see Gen. 32:24–31) or
Jesus praying so fervently in the garden of Gethsemane that His
sweat became like drops of blood (see Luke 22:41–44). What was
so important that Epaphras would pray this fervently? That the
Colossian church would grow in their knowledge of God's will and
in maturity of faith.

God likewise calls us to prayer for ourselves and for His church.
We would all be encouraged to reflect on these simple questions:
"What would You do through me, Lord, to work Your will in my
life and in the church? How would you have me invest in the work
of Your kingdom?" This means prayerfully wrestling with God
over this matter. Such prayer exercises our faith. The struggle to

respond faithfully is not, nor should it be, easy. Colossians 4:13 goes on to describe Epaphras this way: "I vouch for him that he is working hard for you" (NIV).

The church needs an Epaphras or two. The church needs people who will pray earnestly to seek God's will for the church's direction, for their own involvement in it, for those who don't yet know Christ. Are you willing to pray, to wrestle hard, for the kingdom of God and the destiny of lives hanging in the balance? Decide now to make a prayerful decision about your participation in the ministry of the church and the kingdom of God.

PRAYER

Lord, lead me in prayer to wrestle hard regarding Your will. I will hold fast to You until I find Your blessing. Remind me that my journey with You is also a battle. I hunger to surrender to You and Your heart for me and others. Holy Spirit, move over my thoughts and the intent of my heart. Amen.

DAY 76

....

Learn to Worship Deeply

I will not offer burnt offerings to
the LORD my God which cost me nothing.

2 SAMUEL 24:24

When we grow into God's heart, something divine happens in us: we come to understand that worship involves sacrifice. Worship takes on so many different looks: raising our hands when we sing, kneeling before our Father, feeding the hungry, or giving our money. But all these things have one thing in common: they cost us something. And they only happen joyfully when we are in love with God.

David makes a statement in 2 Samuel that rattles my cage. He understood his Father's heart: best and first come not out of demand but out of affection. God does not ask us to give because He needs our resources or because He is demanding. He asks us to give because He wants our hearts.

Any gift, whether of our money, time, or talents, will make a difference to the kingdom of God, but it also makes a huge difference in us. Through such a gift God will actually grow our faith and commitment. David was offered a gift to help him make his sacrifice for free, which could have been tempting, but he refused

165

because he understood the principles of partnering with and giving to God. His heart had to be in the gift.

Such a gift will certainly cost us something. As we saw earlier, King David had an opportunity to make an easy sacrifice, or offering, to God. Araunah was going to give him the whole deal—the threshing floor (the place for the altar), the oxen, and even the wood for the sacrifice—for nothing. What a deal! But David realized that such a deal was really no sacrifice for himself at all; there was no first or best in that type of offering, no worship that honored his Lord and God. "I will not offer burnt offerings to the LORD my God which cost me nothing," David said.

Offering ourselves to God, or giving sacrificially, does not come easily. As I said before, it will cost us something. Does your giving model the kind of commitment that would honor and worship God? Does your sacrifice make a real difference in how you live? Are you giving in ways that shape your living? If you can answer yes, then you are not simply sharing a gift—you are sharing your life and your faith.

PRAYER

Jesus, teach me that giving my firstfruits and my best offering will bring me life. If I give myself in ways that mean little to me, how will that honor and worship You? Let my giving honor You as my Lord and my God. Amen.

....

Yielding to God's Heart

To one he gave five talents, to another, two, and to another, one,
each according to his own ability; and he went on his journey.

MATTHEW 25:15

This little story found in Matthew 25:14–30 gives us a huge look into how our heavenly Father views us as His kids. He treats us with a ton of respect by always allowing us a choice in the matters of life. He doesn't force us to love others; He asks us to. He doesn't force us to put Him first; He asks us to. He doesn't make us serve Him; He asks us to.

For some of us, serving comes far more naturally than it does for others. Some of us are born doers, while others are not. But in this parable it is clear that God expects all of us to use our gifts for His glory. God has given each of us a mind, physical strength, and a will. What we do with these each day will determine how deeply we grow in Him. If we see our skills as something we develop and own, then we will rarely use them to serve others. But if we realize that all the gifts and talents we have are God given, then we become keenly aware that they belong to Him, not us. This makes using them to serve others much more likely—and much more life giving.

In the parable of the talents, Jesus clearly states that all our talents come from Him and that we are responsible to use them and see them multiply. Digging a hole and burying what God has given us is not a good idea, because He will hold us accountable for how we use our gifts and talents. Jesus expects us to take risks in our serving of others. Reaching out of our comfort zone is always scary, but it is a life principle that is not an option.

Is it a gamble to engage in what the Holy Spirit leads us to do each day? Absolutely. That is clear in this parable. Life is risky, but doing nothing is not an option. Take a risk every day with the gifts and talents God has imparted to you, because, as Jesus says toward the end of the story, "to everyone who has, more shall be given, and he will have an abundance; but from the one who does not have, even what he does have shall be taken away" (Matt. 25:29).

—◌ PRAYER ◌—

Holy Spirit, You impart spiritual gifts to all those who know Jesus, and I am sure when You give me those gifts, You want me to use them for Jesus' glory. Teach me to obey You when You ask me to move, even if it is uncomfortable for me. I want to be a wise and faithful servant who pleases You. Thank You, Father. Amen.

DAY 78

A Little Sacrifice Can Go a Long Way

Instruct those who are rich in this present world . . . to do good,
to be rich in good works, to be generous and ready to share,
storing up for themselves the treasure of a good foundation for the
future, so that they may take hold of that which is life indeed.

1 TIMOTHY 6:17-19

Most of us wouldn't consider ourselves rich. But take a trip to a Cambodian province, and we might feel like billionaires.

A few years ago, Pastor Jesse McCall from New Life Church in Phnom Pen, Cambodia, took me and several other Water of Life leaders to a church they had planted near the Vietnamese border. When we arrived at the church in this small village, I saw a bunch of young people playing volleyball. Jesse explained that this was a regular outreach. I didn't see the pastor of the church, however, so Jesse went to find him.

When the pastor showed up, Jesse explained that he didn't like being around the villagers, as some had begun to taunt his faith because his wife worked in a sweatshop. She rode the bus seven days a week, two hours each way, and worked a twelve-hour shift, except Sundays, when she worked eight hours. People were asking the pastor, "If your God is really God, why does she have to work like that?"

I was stunned. This family had two small children under seven and a mother who was gone sixteen hours a day so her husband could pastor a church. I asked Pastor Jesse how much money she made, and he said, "One hundred twenty-one dollars."

"A week?" I asked.

"No, a month!" he answered. Now let's talk about who's rich.

First Timothy 6:18 tells us "to be generous and ready to share." I quickly added up the numbers in my head and figured that for 3,600 dollars this lady could stay home for three years. I told our leaders, and before you knew it, we had 3,600 dollars on the spot. When we gave it to the pastor, I had Pastor Jesse ask him, "If we paid for three years of your wife's salary, would she quit tomorrow?" He looked bewildered. Pastor Jesse explained to him what we wanted to do, and he said yes, she would quit tomorrow.

We gave the money to New Life Church so they could add it to his salary each month, and we loaded up in the van to leave. As we were about to close the door, the Cambodian pastor came up and laid his hand on my arm with tears in his eyes. We didn't speak the same language, but the message was clear: "I don't know how to thank you, but I am so grateful."

Be generous. Live under your means, not beyond them. Learn to give when you have a little, and God will use you to give a lot. We were created to bless others after our Father blesses us. Learn generosity by giving, and store up for yourselves riches in eternity!

⟶ PRAYER ⟵

Father, I have so much. Teach me to be generous, to give to others, and to live below my means, not above them. Thank You for being so generous to me. You gave Your Son. Please remind me of that each time You ask me to give. Amen.

DAY 79

....

Giving Brings Joy!

Give, and it will be given to you. A good measure, pressed down,
shaken together and running over, will be poured into your lap.
For with the measure you use, it will be measured to you.

LUKE 6:38, NIV

Luke 6:38 is an amazing verse. What a promise Jesus makes to us in it: "Give, and I will give to you." When we give of ourselves joyfully, we position ourselves to receive blessings from above. As Jack Hayford said, "Joyous, praise-filled giving (born of prayer and the Spirit instead of promotion and the systems) brings great giving alive and propels its possibilities of release forward."[2]

Giving is to our spiritual lives what water is to our physical lives. Without giving we will ultimately die: "Remember this: Whoever sows sparingly will also reap sparingly, and whoever sows generously will also reap generously. Each of you should give what you have decided in your heart to give, not reluctantly or under compulsion, for God loves a cheerful giver" (2 Cor. 9:6-7, NIV). Joy is a byproduct of a generous heart. Since God promises to supply all our need, giving to others a portion of what He has provided us brings joy to us and blessing to others.

It is easy for us to slip into a mind-set of mediocrity. Life is so busy, and just surviving the day to day can be tough. But essential to growing deep spiritually is a lifestyle of excellence. When President John F. Kennedy made the famous statement, "Ask not what your country can do for you—ask what you can do for your country,"[3] he was challenging a mind-set that is self-centered and shallow. Self-preservation can seem so much more practical than self-sacrifice, but the Bible teaches the opposite.

When Mary poured out a year's worth of work in the form of precious perfume to anoint Jesus, most of those present didn't see her act of devotion as wise but as wasteful. But to their astonishment, Jesus praised the woman and her extravagant gift and proclaimed that she would be remembered forever in history (see Mark 14:9). Wow, talk about a reversal!

Jesus gave His best for us. His gift too was extravagant and costly, and He calls us to give as He did: "Live a life filled with love, following the example of Christ. He loved us and offered himself as a sacrifice for us, a pleasing aroma to God" (Eph. 5:2, NLT).

Are you sacrificial, willing to put others before yourself? Do you give of your time, talent, and resources to bring life to others? If serving others is difficult for you, remember that God has challenged us to see if we can out-give Him (see Mal. 3:10). All our resources really belong to Him; trust Him, and you'll find that giving will become a joyous part of your life.

⸺ PRAYER ⸺

Lord, make me a joyous giver, one who will be like You—free to give and free to receive. Help me not to view giving as a duty but rather a blessing. Holy Spirit, work Your deep work in my heart. I need to be transformed from a taker into a giver, and You are the One who can do that! Thank You. Amen.

DAY 80

Living for Others

The only thing that counts is faith expressing itself through love.

GALATIANS 5:6, NIV

The journey of faith is about learning to walk deeply with Jesus and care for others. First John 3:17–18 speaks directly to the issue: "If someone has enough money to live well and sees a brother or sister in need but shows no compassion—how can God's love be in that person? Dear children, let's not merely say that we love each other; let us show the truth by our actions" (NLT).

The love of God is not a feeling or a thought—it's an action. Talk is cheap. That may sound harsh, but when it comes to kingdom living, it's true. All our good intentions, promises, and resolutions mean nothing; they must turn into actions. In the same way, the love of Christ means nothing to the people around us if we don't demonstrate it. The Message puts it well: "Let's not just talk about love; let's practice real love" (1 John 3:18). Saying we care for someone and showing love to that person are entirely different things, according to James 2:15–17:

> Suppose you see a brother or sister who has no food or clothing, and you say, "Good-bye and have a good day; stay warm and eat well"—but then you don't give that person any food or clothing. What good does that do? So you see, faith by itself isn't enough. Unless it produces good deeds, it is dead and useless. (NLT)

This takes sacrifice, doesn't it? But because God loves us deeply, He wants to use us to touch others.

How can we become truly loving people? First, we must rely on God's command to love to give us the confidence that we *can* love! The challenge to love is not just another burden to load us down with—it is God's promise to us!

Second, we must look always at Jesus' love for us. To love, we must know that we are loved. Every day we should thank God for His great love. It keeps us focused on the source of love: Jesus.

Third, we must aim higher than the world around us. The love of the world says, "I love you because you love me," or, "You do something for me," or, "I have to love you." God's love is different. He loves simply because He *is* love. It's God's love for us that gives us the strength to truly love one another.

Walking with God is sometimes difficult, but it is full of hope, love, and faith—hope to change a generation, love to fuel our fires, and faith to move mountains for our King. God is calling us to live extraordinary lives. The time to do that is not next year or next month or even tomorrow. The time is now. Share your gifts and your resources with others today. Don't limit yourself. Make a difference! Seize the day for the King and the kingdom.

PRAYER

Dear Lord, only Your Spirit can help me love others. Send Your Spirit to me that I might be able to love others more perfectly. Thank You, Father. Amen.

DAY 81

Excess Baggage

Every branch that bears fruit,
[God] prunes it so that it may bear more fruit.

JOHN 15:2

Our garages can accumulate stuff. If we live in the same house for very long, we will notice how much we gather. Life is like that. We allow things to accumulate in our hearts that really have no significance, but they take up space in our lives. Jesus understands that if we don't cut some of that junk out, it will bog us down.

Maybe we need to be cut back in some overgrown areas of our lives in order to bear better fruit for God's kingdom. Grapevines naturally overextend themselves with prolific branching and leaf growth every year. If grapevines are not pruned, their growth can completely cover an arbor in as little as two growing seasons. Unchecked branching growth, while great for simply covering up space in a yard, is terrible for bearing fruit. Such overgrown grapevines will bear tiny, unusable fruit—if they are able to bear fruit clusters at all. The extensive branching and leafing drains the resources and energy of the vine from its primary purpose: bearing fruit. In a well-kept vineyard, whose purpose is to bear good fruit, are thick, decades-old grapevines pruned back to no more than four short branches so that all the energy of the plant is focused on growing great grapes. Heavy, regular pruning is necessary to bearing good fruit.

How overextended is your life? What things have you branched out into? We may think that wildly branching out everywhere as fast as we can helps us cover all the bases in life, but in truth, such unmanaged growth keeps us from bearing any real fruit. Where can you cut back so you can invest the time and energy and resources available to you into bearing the kind of good fruit in your life that matters? What branches can you cut out? What resources does that pruning free up for you to invest in bearing good fruit?

If it has been awhile since you paid any attention to pruning, you may be astonished as to how overgrown and overextended your life has become—a bit like an overly stuffed garage! No wonder Jesus says that God will prune our lives to help us bear better fruit.

PRAYER

Lord, abide more fully in me. Teach me to abide in You and allow You to prune me. Show me the areas in my life that You want me to prune and manage better. Reshape my living so that I can bear good fruit that will glorify You. Thank You, Father. Amen.

DAY 82

....

Give God the Glory

Praise be to you, LORD, the God of our father Israel,
from everlasting to everlasting. . . . Yours, LORD, is the greatness and
the power and the glory and the majesty and the splendor. . . .
We give You thanks, and praise Your glorious name.

1 CHRONICLES 29:10-13

We get the sense that David could have gone on and on about God's blessings and glory and greatness. When God touches our situation with favor and we see His hand on us, it is vital for us to praise and honor Him. But it is so human for us to take things for granted, isn't it? Why is it that we so quickly forget all that God has done for us?

Holy Spirit-assisted praise and prayer are vitally important. It helps us remember our Father's goodness and brings us back to an attitude of humility and gratefulness. Giving God His rightful place in praise will position us under the Father's hand to receive renewed life and love from Jesus so that we can be a blessing to others, that they too may glorify Him!

When we begin to live in God's favor, life can get really interesting. We are not nearly as affected by the opinions of others as we were before. Most of all, doors begin to open to us that we could never have opened on our own. The question is, will we lose our way? Many of us do, and we never grow deeper with the Lord.

See, we didn't choose Him; He chose us. And when He did, He told us that He expected us to grow and bear fruit for Him:

"You didn't choose me. I chose you. I appointed you to go and produce lasting fruit, so that the Father will give you whatever you ask for, using my name. This is my command: Love each other" (John 15:16–17). Favor is given to us so that we can answer God's call to inspire, influence, and impact our world by serving Him and others.

When you see God's hand on you, stop and tell Him thanks. Ask the Holy Spirit to assist your time of praise and prayer (see Jude 20) and bring to your remembrance all that Jesus has done for you and in you. Keep things straight here—God can do His work without us, but He chooses to walk with us and to use us. Enjoy His favor, and remember where it came from! He gives blessing and favor to those who seek Him first.

—◌ PRAYER ◌—

Father, forgive me for failing to acknowledge Your hand in my circumstances. Help me see all that You do to bring life to me. Assist me, Holy Spirit, in my daily worship of Jesus, and bring to my mind thoughts of His goodness and love for me. Release me to worship Him freely and boldly as David did. Thank You, Lord. Amen.

DAY 83

The Seed Principle

*Do not be deceived, God is not mocked; for whatever a man sows,
this he will also reap. For the one who sows to his own flesh will from
the flesh reap corruption, but the one who sows to the Spirit will
from the Spirit reap eternal life.*

GALATIANS 6:7-8

Many of us think that it's easy to pull one over on God, that
somehow we can slip one by Him. This is way beyond foolish—it is blind pride. The warning Paul wrote in Galatians 6:7 to
the church in Galatia was clear: "Do not be deceived, God is not
mocked." Paul was saying that when God implements a life principle, it can never be changed by man. The particular life principle
he was referring to is this: things multiply after their kind. If we
sow wheat, we will yield wheat; if we sow corn, we will have corn as
our product. Likewise, if we sow anger, we will reap anger; if we sow
kindness, we will reap kindness.

We reap what we sow. This is God's order of things, which naturally implies that if we do not sow, then we cannot reap. Jesus
taught this lesson:

> The kingdom of God is like a man who casts seed upon the
> soil; and he goes to bed at night and gets up by day, and the
> seed sprouts and grows—how, he himself does not know.
> The soil produces crops by itself; first the blade, then the
> head, then the mature grain in the head. But when the crop

permits, he immediately puts in the sickle, because the harvest has come. (Mark 4:26–29)

The implication is real: a man sows seed, and he gets a crop. He doesn't know how this happens, but it does. What if he never plants a seed? He will have no crop.

Do you realize that each day we are planting seeds? The question is, what kind—love, life, healing, hope or jealousy, unforgiveness, and bitterness? Whatever we sow we will reap. Whatever we plant today we will reap down the road.

How does this happen? We don't understand it all, like the farmer in Jesus' story, but we can be sure that it is true, because God has set it as a principle of life. Sow life into others, and we will get life from Jesus. Remember, being faithful with little yields much. Put your little seeds in the ground, and God can grow faith in your heart.

PRAYER

Father, today I desire to sow life into others. Please fill me with seeds of hope and life, Holy Spirit, and then teach me and lead me as I plant those seeds into others' lives and circumstances wherever I go today. Amen.

DAY 84

The Principle
of Multiplication

*To Him who is able to do far more abundantly beyond all
that we ask or think, according to the power that works within us,
to Him be the glory in the church and in Christ Jesus
to all generations forever and ever. Amen.*

EPHESIANS 3:20-21

A certain principle always partners with sowing and reaping in Christ. Yes, we sow and then we reap, but it's also true that we always reap *more* than we sow. This is the principle of multiplication. God is able to take what little we give Him and multiply it for His glory. Sometimes we feel so feeble and weak, as if we will never make a difference in the kingdom of God. We feel small and insignificant, and maybe we actually are. But God is not, and He is able to take what we sow for Him and multiply it for His glory.

Remember the story of the loaves and fishes? That is the principle. In that story Jesus did something remarkable—He multiplied someone's offering:

He said to them, "How many loaves do you have? Go look!" And when they found out, they said, "Five, and two fish." And He commanded them all to sit down by groups on the green grass. They sat down in groups of hundreds and of fifties. And He took the five loaves and the two fish, and looking up toward heaven, He blessed the food and broke the loaves and He kept giving them to the disciples to set before them; and He divided up the two fish among them all. They all ate and were satisfied, and they picked up twelve full baskets of the broken pieces, and also of the fish. There were five thousand men who ate the loaves. (Mark 6:38–44)

However insignificant you seem to be, never forget that Jesus can take whatever you give Him and multiply it a thousand times over into others' lives. Never think small! Believe big! Our God is huge, and He will multiply your seed: "Those who sow in tears shall reap with joyful shouting. He who goes to and fro weeping, carrying his bag of seed, shall indeed come again with a shout of joy, bringing his sheaves with him" (Ps. 126:5–6).

—⸱ PRAYER ⸱—

Father, You can do more than I could ever ask or think. Teach me, Lord, to trust You to take my little offering and multiply it into greatness for Your glory. Use me to touch people in ways I never imagined I could. Thank You! Amen.

What Are You Sowing?

I, the LORD, search the heart, I test the mind, even to give to each man according to his ways, according to the results of his deeds.

JEREMIAH 17:10

The Bible is full of principles that on the surface make absolutely no sense to us, but when we look at them with eyes of faith, they become very clear. God is in the business of building faith in us, so often He will do things exactly the opposite of how you or I might do them. If we approach His kingdom with a faith perspective, things will fall right into place; but if we come attempting to reason with God on human terms, we will be pretty frustrated.

Take this principle, for example, that we examined earlier: "Give, and it will be given to you. A good measure, pressed down, shaken together and running over, will be poured into your lap. For with the measure you use, it will be measured to you" (Luke 6:38, NIV). This verse reveals a principle that applies to every area of our lives. It is the principle that will determine whether we grow into givers or remain takers our whole lives. We are all born takers; being selfish is quite natural for most of us. It takes learning to live out of our Father's heart to make us givers.

The verses before the one quoted in the previous paragraph state, "Be merciful, just as your Father is merciful. Do not judge, and you will not be judged. Do not condemn, and you will not be condemned. Forgive, and you will be forgiven" (Luke 6:36–37, NIV). If we sow love, we will receive an overflowing harvest of love. If we forgive, we will be forgiven. If we extend grace, we will receive God's grace. This is certainly upside down compared to what the world teaches, but these principles give us life.

Whatever we sow we will reap. So what is it that you are sowing? This is a vital question to answer, because we are all sowing something—the only question is what? Is it life giving or not? Is it born out of Jesus' heart or our own?

PRAYER

Jesus, give me Your heart. When I live according to Your Spirit in me, I am a giver, and my Father's heart flows freely toward others. But when I insist on my own way, I am always a taker. Heal me of selfishness, and empower me today to break the selfish stranglehold that grips my heart. Thank You, Lord! Amen.

Character Supports Destiny

*His master's wife looked with desire at Joseph, and she said,
"Lie with me." But he refused and said to his master's wife,
"Behold, with me here, my master does not concern himself with
anything in the house, and he has put all that he owns in my charge.
There is no one greater in this house than I, and he has
withheld nothing from me except you, because you are his wife.
How then could I do this great evil and sin against God?"*

GENESIS 39:7-9

If we are going to partner with God in the work of the kingdom, we must grow in godly character. Without character we will have no destiny. We are all tempted by the world, the flesh, and the enemy, but if we surrender to our passions, we lose our possibility.

When we draw near to Jesus daily, He guards, corrects, and protects our lives. He keeps us on track so we don't lose our way. When we fail to draw near to Him, we are vulnerable to the temptations around us, the ones that shipwreck our faith and ruin our hearts and character. Many of us hunger for God's touch in our journey, but we refuse His correction. If we let God correct us, however, we grow in character. Character supports our destinies and positions us for the Holy Spirit to move in and through us with power.

It is human to pursue power, money, and things. Coming to grips with what we are as humans is so important to growing spiritually. Some people seem so set on acting as if they have no issues, no shortcomings, no weaknesses. But every one of us has struggled with a desire to compromise, lie, cheat, or steal at one time or another. If we are going to be transformed by Jesus and useful in His service, then we'd better learn to be honest about this. Change is hard enough, but lying to ourselves will make it impossible.

Most of us tend to default, at some point, back to our pasts. A study of two thousand heart-bypass patients who survived at least two years following surgery shockingly revealed that 90 percent of them reverted back to the same lifestyle habits that had gotten them into health crises in the first place; even when faced with death, they didn't make necessary changes. I am like that—aren't you? But God wants to transform us by renewing our thinking; Romans 12:2 is clear about that. Without the Holy Spirit's power working in us daily, we are dust! But when He is at work, we are super conquerors—able to take what was meant for evil and allow God to turn it to good.

Let Jesus shape your character every day and every moment, and see what He will do through you to touch others and invest in His kingdom.

—◦ PRAYER ◦—

Jesus, each time I am tempted to stray, stop me and convict me. Correct me, please. I desire to be holy. I know that my character counts and that the decisions I make each day impact my destiny. Draw me to You, and teach me that Your Holy Spirit is the power I need to walk uprightly. Amen.

DAY 87

....

Failure Doesn't Have to Define You

*My son, I had intended to build a house to the name of
the LORD my God. But the word of the LORD came to me, saying,
"You have shed much blood and have waged great wars; you shall
not build a house to My name, because you have shed so much
blood on the earth before Me."*

1 CHRONICLES 22:7-8

While God wants to draw us deep into His heart, the fact is that failure is real for all of us at times. We hate to fail, and often when we do, we allow the failure to shape our view of ourselves, sometimes to the point that it begins to become our identity. What we do with our failure, however, determines if it will build us or break us. The Bible is full of stories of people who failed at marriage, decision making, relationships—on and on the list could go. Yet many of those same people became world changers, like David.

When you fail, does it shape your identity in a negative way? Do you begin to think that you really are a loser? David, for all his greatness, was also a massive failure. In fact, I don't know any person who is viewed as successful who has not failed greatly. David hungered to build a temple for God. He wanted that building to be a legacy of his heart toward God. But it wasn't to be because of his past failures.

His failures prevented him from attaining his deep desire. Isn't that just like you and me? We fall and fail, and we lose something we desperately wanted, loved, or needed. But God is bigger than our failures, just as He was bigger than David's. He is faithful to reset our course and redirect our purpose into His hand. This is the promise of Romans 8:28: "God causes all things to work together for good to those who love God, to those who are called according to His purpose."

When we read a verse like this, often we can't get our heads around it, much less get our hearts to believe it. This verse stands as tall as any we find in the entire Bible. It contains everything Jesus brings us—healing, possibility, grace, forgiveness, love, and restoration—all in one short verse. God causes every failure, loss, wound, struggle, and terror in our lives to work something life giving if we will lay it down before Him.

We shouldn't walk out on God when we fail but rather lean in to Him, realizing as David did that our failures don't change God's heart of favor toward us. His heart is not built on what we do but on who He is. Whatever you are dealing with, learn from David. Run to God, and let Him put the pieces back together again. He is way better at that than you or I will ever be.

⸺᠗ Prayer ᠗⸻

Jesus, please do not allow me to live unhappily in my failures. Far too often You forgive me long before I forgive myself. I desire for my identity to be shaped by Your view of me, not by my view of my failures. Thank You, Holy Spirit, for being so healing in my life. Amen.

DAY 88

....

Find Your Glass
Half Full

When your days are complete and you lie down with your fathers,
I will raise up your descendant after you, who will come forth from
you, and I will establish his kingdom. He shall build a house for
My name, and I will establish the throne of his kingdom forever.

2 SAMUEL 7:12-13

When we crash headlong into disappointment, most of us don't stop to give thanks for what we have, because it is so human for us to dwell on what we don't have or what we have lost. David lost a ton when the Lord told him he would not be the one to build the temple. But amazingly, he settled the issue with the Lord and moved ahead, making the best out of what he had and not dwelling on what he had lost. This is a grand trait that would serve many of us well if we would allow ourselves to embrace the part of our lives that God is rescuing for us and not remain mired in what we have lost.

Second Samuel tells this story with a slightly different twist than 1 Chronicles does. God reminded David of where he had come from: he had been a lowly shepherd boy who had become king. Perspective sure can help when we are in the midst of disappointment. Only after reminding David of his life's blessing did God break the news to him that it would be his son, not him, who would build God a house:

189

I took you from the pasture, from tending the sheep, and appointed you ruler over my people Israel. I have been with you wherever you have gone, and I have cut off all your enemies from before you. Now I will make your name great, like the names of the greatest men on earth.... When your days are over and you rest with your ancestors, I will raise up your offspring to succeed you, your own flesh and blood, and I will establish his kingdom. He is the one who will build a house for my Name, and I will establish the throne of his kingdom forever. (2 Sam. 7:8–13)

So many great leaders in the Bible faced exactly the same kinds of huge disappointments we do: Moses was told he wouldn't make it into the promised land; Joseph was sold as a slave and separated from his family; Ruth's husband died, and her world was shattered. But God can heal us. He knows our loss and disappointment, and He is bigger than both.

Don't hold on to hurt and grow bitter. Relent as David did, and embrace the journey as the twists and turns come. Surrender to God, and let Him heal the situation on His terms, His way. He will prosper you, and His blessings will flow in you once again.

PRAYER

Father, You are all-wise, and I often forget that in my day-to-day battles. I want to declare to You that I trust Your way. I embrace Your healing in my disappointment. Move in on me, Holy Spirit, with Your comfort and assurance, and teach me that You can heal my disappointment and make life flow again. Amen.

DAY 89

....

No Excuses

A man was giving a big dinner, and he invited many;
and at the dinner hour he sent his slave to say to those
who had been invited, "Come; for everything is ready now."
But they all alike began to make excuses.

LUKE 14:16-18

How many reasons are there for *not* participating in the work of God's kingdom? The possibilities are endless! There are more than enough reasons to justify anyone.

A modern parable might begin like this:

> The kingdom of God is like a modern local church. God gave His people a vision. "Come," said God, "and take the place prepared for you. Take up your part in My work. Everything is ready now. All of you are invited to make a difference! When you take your place and take up your part, all of you will be blessed to break bread in My kingdom." But they all alike began to make excuses.

The most important piece of a jigsaw puzzle is the piece that is missing. Every piece is important to making the whole picture work.

The word "synergy" explains this. It is a word best understood when divided. The prefix *syn* means "together," while *ergo* is Greek for "work." When merged, the words mean "working together." But synergy means more than that. The word fully defined means that the result accomplished by people working together is greater than what could be accomplished by the individual parts. Sports teams demonstrate the meaning of synergy. Playing together makes them better than playing as individuals. It's not the individual talent that results in great things but the work together. Just one team member failing to do his or her part can make everyone lose. It's the same with an orchestra; just one musician not in concert with the others can ruin the music.

Paul calls every Christian to a renewed way of thinking by which we give ourselves wholly to the Lord and His will for us. He calls us to be completely transformed by the renewing of our minds, to give ourselves as living and holy sacrifices (see Rom. 12:1–2) as members of the body of Christ. Do people notice that your life is molded by the mind of Christ? Can anyone see your transformation? How has your life of faith changed your mind? How have your priorities changed? Are you still conformed to this world, or is your mind being transformed? Can anyone notice the difference in you as you offer yourself more fully to God alongside others who love Jesus?

Your participation in the mission of God's kingdom is unquestionably significant. No one can play your part but you. No one can give your share but you. Others can only do their part. If you have a list of excuses, take that list and offer it up as a burnt sacrifice. Then ask God to show you why the expansion of the kingdom is important to His heart and help you discover reasons you can serve in that expansion.

—⌒ PRAYER ⌒—

Lord, when Your call challenges me, it is easy for me to excuse myself. Reach me! Compel me to respond to Your call in whatever ways I can. Teach me that synergy in Your kingdom is about *me*! Thank You for including me in Your work, Lord. Amen.

DAY 90

....

Investing in Eternity

*By working hard in this manner you must help the weak
and remember the words of the Lord Jesus, that He Himself said,
"It is more blessed to give than to receive."*

ACTS 20:35

Eternity changes everything. We are not called just to live out our existence here on Earth and then move on. Our time on Earth is preparation for our time in eternity. Jesus said that we would prepare for eternity by caring for the weak and the poor (see Matt. 25:31–46). If all we have is this life, then we'd better use our resources for that new car and a bigger house. But if we believe in an eternity that awaits God's people, then eternal issues should be infinitely more important to us in the long run.

Wise stewards recognize this. They understand that things will eventually wear out and break, so they don't set their mind on them. They set their mind on things of eternity, as Paul told us to do: "Set your mind on the things above, not on the things that are on earth" (Col. 3:2).

If we are going to be wise stewards, we should look for ways to maximize our resources for the kingdom of God. We need an eternal perspective of our stuff. Most of us have accounts in the bank, but we definitely have accounts in heaven. Paul spoke about our heavenly accounts in Philippians 4:14–17: "You have done well to share with me in my affliction. . . . Not that I seek the gift itself, but I seek for the profit which increases to your account."

Jesus painted a powerful picture in Matthew 25:14–30 of how God views our accounts and what we do with them. It is important for us as stewards to remember that when we invest in the kingdom of God, we sow into our accounts by touching others' lives.

When a woman named Helen Lovett left her estate to Water of Life Community Church, she touched more lives than she probably ever could have dreamed. She is touching your life, and she never knew you! Helen couldn't take her estate with her, but as a wise steward, she sent it ahead. She blessed thousands of lives. As a partner with God, you are positioned to do exactly the same thing for the kingdom of God. Pray this through, and give of your life and your resources as the Holy Spirit leads you—no more, no less—and people will be blessed.

PRAYER

Father, thank You for the journey. It is always a blessing to walk with You. You teach me so much about life and living that I would have no understanding of without You. Holy Spirit, please touch my life, and help me sow into my heavenly account by touching thousands of lives for Your glory. Thank You, Jesus. Amen.

Notes

Days 1–30: Positioning Yourself Before God's Throne
1. Kurt A. Richardson, *The New American Commentary: James*, vol. 36 (Nashville: Holman, 1997).
2. Bible Tools, s.v. "Prosperity" (Hebrew *towb*), www.bibletools.org/index.cfm/fuseaction/ Lexicon.show/ID/H2896/towb.htm (accessed October 10, 2017).
3. Lisa Belkin, "Huffpost Poll: What Would You Do With an Extra Hour Every Day?" *HuffPost*, August 2, 2013, www.huffingtonpost.com/2013/08/02/extra-hour-a-day_n_3697387.html (accessed September 26, 2017).

Days 31–60: Stepping Out in Courage and Faith
1. F. B. Meyer, *The Life of Abraham* (Lynnwood, WA: Emerald, 2001), 27.
2. L. B. Cowman, *Streams in the Desert*, ed. Jim Reimann (Grand Rapids: Zondervan, 1999), February 17.
3. Bill Hybels, *The Volunteer Revolution: Unleashing the Power of Everybody* (Grand Rapids: Zondervan, 2004).
4. Andrew Murray, *With Christ in the School of Prayer* (New Kensington, PA: Whitaker, 1985), chap. 12.
5. C. S. Lewis, *The Problem of Pain* (New York: Harper Collins, 1996), 91.
6. Murray, *With Christ in the School of Prayer*, chap. 13.
7. Howard Thurman, source unknown.
8. Murray in David Hazard, *Mighty Is Your Hand: A 40-Day Journey in the Company of Andrew Murray: Devotional Reading Arranged and Paraphrased* (Bloomington, MN: Bethany, 1993).

Days 61–90: Fulfilling Your Destiny
1. The Lord declares that the firstborn are His at least thirteen times: Exodus 13:2, 12; 22:29; 34:19; Leviticus 27:26; Numbers 3:12, 13, 45; 8:16, 17; Deuteronomy 15:19; Luke 2:23; and Hebrews 12:23.
2. Hayford, source unknown.
3. John F. Kennedy, United States presidential inaugural address, January 20, 1961, http://www.ushistory.org/documents/ask-not.htm (accessed October 5, 2017).

About the Author

Dan Carroll grew up in Pomona, California. In February 1970, he received Christ as his savior at a Youth for Christ meeting. In 1976 he received a B.A. in religion from the University of La Verne and went on to teach in the Pomona Unified School District for three years. Then in 1979 he received his M.A. in education from the Claremont Graduate University. Dan and his wife moved to Idaho, where he taught high-school English and history and coached the basketball team. He also served as an elder at Community Fellowship Church.

In 1982 Dan took a youth-pastor position at Life Bible Fellowship in Upland, California, and served there until 1987. He received an M.A. in Christian Ministry from the International School of Theology in 1987.

In 1987 Pastor Dan began teaching a men's Bible study. For three years the study grew in scope and depth, and the families of the men involved began to come together for fellowship. In 1989 Dan and his family went to the Youth With A Mission training school in Kona, Hawaii. They were introduced to cross-cultural ministry in Penang, Malaysia, where Dan received a vision for the world. After returning to the United States in 1990, he was encouraged by the men of his Bible study and their families to plant a church. This became Water of Life Community Church.

Pastor Dan completed a doctorate of ministry from the King's Seminary in 2004. He continues today as the senior pastor of Water of Life Community Church.

Dan and Gale have been married for thirty-nine years and have two adult children, Shane and Katie, who are both married, and three grandsons.

About Water of Life Community Church

Water of Life Community Church is a non-denominational evangelical charismatic church. This means that we are devoted to studying and obeying the Bible, which is the Word of God, and that we believe in the baptism of the Holy Spirit and the modern-day operation of the gifts proclaimed in the New Testament.

Water of Life was established on Sunday, October 28, 1990, when a group of twenty-one adults and eleven children gathered together to worship at the La Petite childcare building in Rancho Cucamonga, California. It was a fellowship that arose from a men's Bible study, a group of people who grew together, and a body that is now committed together to seek God's plan as a church family.

Many people love God but have become disillusioned with the church. Therefore, a church that offers a personal encounter with Jesus Christ and growth in His Word without the clutter of an overly structured environment has great appeal. Because we want to maintain the integrity and purity of our spiritual purpose, we do not have a rigorous structure with multitudes of committees or membership requirements.

Our desire is to walk by faith and in deep trust of our Lord. That is why you will not see us take an offering. Rather, we believe that the giving of tithes and offerings is worship to Jesus Christ and an expression of the relationship between each individual giver and the Lord.

Although Water of Life is a non-denominational church, we consider ourselves a church that is interdependent with the rest of the body of Christ. Our church is governed by our pastors and our elder board. Additionally, our senior pastor is accountable to an outside group of senior pastors from other local churches as well as to an internationally recognized leader from the Foursquare denomination.

Our Core Values

HEALING

Healing is the very starting point of a transformed life. It speaks to maturing people into a closer relationship with Christ, not just to getting better inside. Jesus put a huge value on healing—putting people back together again. Healing of sick, wounded, and broken lives is a high priority to a compassionate and loving God:

> The Spirit of the LORD is upon me, for he has anointed me to bring Good News to the poor. He has sent me to proclaim that captives will be released, that the blind will see, that the oppressed will be set free, and that the time of the LORD's favor has come. (Luke 4:18–19, NLT)

Healing is so important to God that He made it a key part of discipleship, or growing in Jesus. Healing occurred many times in Jesus' ministry, and miracles frequently occurred. But Jesus' healing was not just about making people well physically. Rather, it was to restore them in the kingdom of God, to bring them into a right relationship with God. Ephesians 4:11–13 talks of apostles, prophets, evangelists, pastors, and teachers all having the responsibility "to equip God's people to do his work and build up the church, the body of Christ . . . until we all come to such unity in our faith and knowledge of God's Son that we will be mature in the Lord, measuring up to the full and complete standard of Christ" (4:12–13, NLT). The word "equip," *kartatizo* in Greek, means "to mend, restore and be put back together."

> I will sprinkle clean water on you, and you will be clean. Your filth will be washed away, and you will no longer

worship idols. And I will give you a new heart, and I will put a new spirit in you. I will take out your stony, stubborn heart and give you a tender, responsive heart. And I will put my Spirit in you so you will follow my decrees and be careful to obey my regulations. (Ezek. 36:25-27, NLT)

The goal in all we do must be transformation—that is where winning begins. God has called us into relationship with one another so that we can be healed and then become instruments of His healing.

Blessed be the God and Father of our Lord Jesus Christ, the Father of mercies and God of all comfort, who comforts us in all our affliction so that we will be able to comfort those who are in any affliction with the comfort with which we ourselves are comforted by God. (2 Cor. 1:3-4)

God does not call us to store up what He gives us but to pass it on to others. Transformation occurs in our church's small groups as well as in our healing and recovery groups, in which people can find support, care, prayer, and encouragement.

SENDING

Sending is our second core value. We believe it is foundational to all that God wants to do in us.

Everything about us likes to be comfortable, *but Jesus told us that the way for us to grow is to be stretched out* (*ekteno* in the Greek). We need to get out of our comfort zones.

In Acts 13:1-3 we read that the church in Jerusalem sent Paul and Barnabas out on the first real missionary journey. Their goal was to reproduce the work God had done in them and in other believers by spreading the word of Jesus' love and transforming lives and starting churches. This church-planting model has been followed in various forms ever since. Our desire at Water of Life is to send teams out for short-term exposure on a regular basis and at the same time to train and expose our church to as many cross-cultural types of ministry as possible. This includes those near to us (in our valley) and those far from us (all over the world). In our history we have sent short-term teams to between fifteen and twenty different countries, including Malaysia, Hong Kong, Russia, China, Jamaica, Venezuela, Guatemala, Lebanon, Panama, Kenya, Nicaragua, El Salvador, Cuba, and Honduras. More recently, we have sent teams to Mexico, Cambodia, and Thailand.

Jesus told His disciples in Matthew 28:19, "Go therefore and make disciples of all the nations, baptizing them in the name of the Father and the Son and the Holy Spirit." In Acts 1:4–8 He told them more:

> Gathering them together, He commanded them not to leave Jerusalem, but to wait for what the Father had promised, "Which," He said, "you heard of from Me; for John baptized with water, but you will be baptized with the Holy Spirit not many days from now." So when they had come together, they were asking Him, saying, "Lord, is it at this time You are restoring the kingdom to Israel?" He said to them, "It is not for you to know times or epochs which the Father has fixed by His own authority; but you will receive power when the Holy Spirit has come upon you; and you shall be My witnesses both in Jerusalem, and in all Judea and Samaria, and even to the remotest part of the earth.

Jerusalem and Judea were home to Jesus and the disciples—that is, local. So we likewise do local outreach at our food-and-clothing warehouse, with our mobile medical unit, and with our annual Trunk-or-Treat Halloween-alternative event. The remote parts of the world for Water of Life are Cambodia and Thailand as well as other nations we have reached. This outreach is all based on Holy Spirit empowerment, and we seek to establish long-term relationships in each of these areas. This will result in transformed lives—in us as we go and in others as they receive.

EQUIPPING

And He gave some as apostles, and some as prophets, and some as evangelists, and some as pastors and teachers, for the equipping of the saints for the work of service, to the building up of the body of Christ. (Eph. 4:11–12)

This core value, like the ones before it, speaks to transforming lives. At Water of Life *winning* is defined as "a transformed life demonstrated by a person being given to God and given to other people." In regard to equipping, as we at Water of Life learn the truth in the Word of God, we receive training along with it as to what we are to do with what we learn. Following God is not just about words—it is an action. A changed person is one who loves God and loves people as well as serves God and serves people.

Equipping at Water of Life means more than just attending church or a Bible study: "The things which you have heard from me in the presence of many witnesses, entrust these to faithful men who will be able to teach others also" (2 Tim. 2:2).

At Water of Life, equipping means teaching and releasing people with the purpose of both mind transformation and heart transformation. Practically speaking, all our small groups will teach and do outreach ministry in which they extend themselves to others. Individuals as well are provided with the opportunity to serve by caring for others—putting their knowledge to work to give life to other people.

CARING

What use is it, my brethren, if someone says he has faith but
has no works? Can that faith save him? If a brother or sister
is without clothing and in need of daily food, and one of you
says to them, "Go in peace, be warmed and be filled," and yet
you do not give them what is necessary for their body, what
use is that? Even so faith, if it has no works, is dead, being by
itself. (James 2:14–17)

We believe that one of Water of Life's main priorities is to care for
those in need. The principle is this: we get so we can give. We believe
this is a part of God's heart for all people. We need the poor and
downtrodden as much as they need us. It is through them that we
gain the heart of God and the Holy Spirit is able to soften us and
impart the Father's heart to us.

The Bible is emphatic about the church's responsibility to care
for those in need: "Whoever has the world's goods, and sees his
brother [or sister] in need and closes his heart against him, how does
the love of God abide in him?" (1 John 3:17).

In Matthew 25 we read that Jesus expects nothing less from His
church, which is why this core value is so important at Water of Life.

This expectation is clearly shown in Scripture:

Then the King will say to those on His right, "Come, you who
are blessed of My Father, inherit the kingdom prepared for
you from the foundation of the world. For I was hungry, and
you gave Me something to eat; I was thirsty, and you gave Me
something to drink; I was a stranger, and you invited Me in;
naked, and you clothed Me; I was sick, and you visited Me; I
was in prison, and you came to Me." (Matt. 25:34–36)

We want to be counted among the faithful described above
as those who fed the hungry, gave drink to the thirsty, invited the

stranger in, clothed the naked, cared for the sick, and also visited those in prison. "The King will answer and say to them, 'Truly I say to you, to the extent that you did it to one of these brothers of Mine, even the least of them, you did it to Me" (Matt. 25:40).

RELATIONSHIPS

Lives are transformed through relationships—community and family relationships: "You are citizens along with all of God's holy people. You are members of God's family. . . . We [who believe] are carefully joined together in him, becoming a holy temple for the Lord" (Eph. 2:19, 21, NLT).

Everyone who believes in Jesus is part of His family. He has joined us together, and He tells us that we should get along. He is the One who holds everything together. He holds the world together, He holds marriages together, He holds the church family together, and He holds personal relationships together: "He is before all things, and in Him all things hold together" (Col. 1:17).

First Corinthians is quite clear in telling us that He put all of us together; we are one body, and we are supposed to live as if we are:

> For even as the body is one and yet has many members, and all the members of the body, though they are many, are one body, so also is Christ. For by one Spirit we were all baptized into one body, whether Jews or Greeks, whether slaves or free, and we were all made to drink of one Spirit. (1 Cor. 12:12–13)

The rules of the family of God are clear and simple: we are called to serve one another. This is only possible through our relationship with Jesus. To have a powerful and on-fire relationship with Jesus, we have to get our mind off ourselves and choose to focus on other people. Christ always did this. He built His relationships with many people based on compassion, and He asks us to do the same. In Mark 1:41, as Jesus spoke with a leper, He was "moved with compassion." He stretched out His hand, touched the leper, and healed him. In order for us to be really connected with others at a deep level, we must be compassionate.

The heart of a servant is a heart of compassion. There is power in serving others, and there is also blessing in serving others. As we come together in right relationship with other people, we position ourselves to be blessed by God.

CONTACT US AT:

Water of Life Community Church
7625 East Avenue, Fontana, CA, 92336
Water of Life Administration Office
14418 Miller Avenue, Suite K, Fontana, CA 92336
Phone: 909.463.0103
Fax: 909.463.1436
E-mail: info@wateroflifecc.org